community |kəˈmjunədi|

noun

• a body of people or things viewed collectively

• a group of people living in the same place or having particular characteristics or interests in common.

Oxford English Dictionary, 3rd Ed.

IN THIS ISSUE

LA+ COMMUNITY
EDITORIAL

The experience of modernity is such that we are each part of many different communities each bound by different forms of association with different rights and rituals. The original type of human community was of course a clan or tribe, no more than say around 100 people held together by constant face-to-face contact. But as numbers swelled, more elaborate forms of bonding were necessary; cities, gods, nations, and not least of all political ideologies. As Garret Dash Nelson explains, and all the authors in this issue explore in different but related ways, any notion of community is at once social, geographic, and political.

Each community in which we participate is a constituent part of our how we construct our individual identities. We must constantly balance and negotiate the existential risks of being too much a part of any one community, or inversely, not enough of any. This is the sliding scale of modern community – the disorientation and liberty of the global city (*gesellschaft*) on the one hand, and the myopia and security of the neighborhood (*gemeinschaft*) at the other. But in a postmodern world where the local and the global are now enveloped into one another like a Klein bottle, locating oneself along such a continuum is not so clear cut. Indeed, as regular contributor philosopher Mark Kingwell alludes, community shouldn't be a simple thing, for otherwise its boundaries calcify leaving us with only two possibilities: in or out. And we all know where that ends up.

The fulcrum for this issue is the optimistic story of Anne Spirn's long-term engagement with the Mill Creek community in West Philadelphia. This, along with the insights from seven BIPOC design justice advocates interviewed by Allison Nkwocha is testament to the rewards of community engagement that is deep and genuine. More and more we see Spirn's legacy in this regard manifesting in a new generation of activist practices of which Kate Orff's SCAPE–interviewed herein–is surely a leading example. Also in Philadelphia, though on the other side of the tracks, planning historian Francesca Ammon teases out the contradictions in the canonical urban renewal success story of Society Hill.

In response to this we can turn to the long-standing champion of public space as the crucible of a tolerant and inclusive society, Julian Agyeman, who sets out the basic theory of what intercultural public space might yet be. By definition, if it is to be inclusive then the design of public space must manifest respect for the marginalized including homeless people, as discussed by James Petty and Alison Young, and people with disabilities, as explored in the essay by Jos Boys. The complicated challenge of achieving equity through the design of public space reaches the scale of a whole city in the case of Los Angeles where Jessica

Henson allows us to get the inside story on the intractably complex socio-political and ecological task of master planning a 51-mile swath of the Los Angeles River with a diverse range of user communities.

As ever in this journal we try to mix theory and practice and maintain an international perspective. This leads us to the extraordinary achievements of the Emscher Park in Germany's Ruhrgebiet where over the last 30 years or so a working-class community facing the trauma of transition to a post-industrial economy, has been in many ways sustained by the medium of landscape, without the forms of displacement or gentrification typically associated with high-end greening. We also hear from Jodi Hilty, the leader of the epic Y2Y project; a 2,500-mile-long conservation corridor between the US and Canada where many different communities with diverse interests are working to come together around a shared sense of place.

Hilty speaks of the importance of Indigenous communities in the creation and maintenance of the Y2Y, a theme extended by Paul Paton and Anne-Marie Pisani in their conversation with Sara Padgett Kjaersgaard about working with Indigenous communities in the Australian context. Crossing to Africa, Chrili Car describes the Guabuliga Green Belt project in Ghana stressing that community engagement is not some form of neocolonial charity or just a means to an end, but the very essence of a project. And to remind us that community engagement is not always meaningful, Mario Matamoros delivers a stinging critique of the way in which developers and their designers in the Honduran city of Tegucigalpa dupe the public with cynical community consultation so as to anesthetize the possibility of dissent.

On the 25th May 2020, as we were already well advanced with this issue, George Floyd was murdered. This stopped us in our tracks and caused us to review what LA+ has done in the past and what it should do in the future. We are proud of the journal's plurality of voices and geographies and also proud of its critical but measured approach to the theory and practice of landscape architecture. That said, we can always do better. We can look beyond our own community and challenge our own identity. Indeed, if you read between the lines in the commentary provided by the seven BIPOC voices who we invited into this issue after Floyd's murder you will find that they are not just asking us to do better, they are asking for fundamental change in how design is taught and practiced.

Tatum L. Hands + Richard Weller
Issue Editors

MARK KINGWELL

Mark Kingwell is a professor of philosophy at the University of Toronto. His most recent books are *On Risk* (2020) and *The Ethics of Architecture* (2021).

✛ PHILOSOPHY

I started thinking about risk and community many months ago, and I have pursued those thoughts at greater length in a short book about risk under pandemic conditions.[1] But the spur of that now-distant moment of first thought, pre-pandemic, was a remark made by Russian President Vladimir Putin in 2019. This was when risk-to-community still meant mainly ideological and perhaps resource-based threats, not primarily epidemiological ones. Mr. Putin said that "the liberal idea has become obsolete."[2] I took this to mean that the putative president-for-life of Russia wanted us to understand that liberal-democratic institutions and the rule of law, at least four centuries in the making but even older in the Roman legal tradition, had been rendered obsolete by the populist-authoritarian movements of the early 21st century. In my mind, the 400-plus years of liberal thought has been about creating community through inclusion of the Other – accommodation of different religions, genders, races, geographies, rather than the exclusion so dominant in other ideas of "community" based on bloodline, cultural uniformity, and shared belief (indeed, most commonly, the shared belief that shared bloodline was even a feature of life).

It strikes me that Putin was correct about then-current "populist" political movements, which were in fact not populist at all but rejections of the liberal idea and hence regressive attacks on the idea of Otherness. The Putin Doctrine (if we can grant such a grandiose title to such a minuscule notion) poses this choice for humanity circa 2020: do you want people to come inside the magic circle of protection and potential affluence, or do you want to keep them out? National borders are the traditional thresholds here, as we were forced to see in Mexico and elsewhere by the depredations of the American president who demanded that a wall be built and also that someone else pay for it. This is fortress America, of course, but much magnified.

Here is how writer Ken Kalfus describes the situation in his brilliant novella *Coup de Foudre* (2015), which fictionalizes Dominique Strauss-Kahn's 2011 sexual assault of a Manhattan hotel housekeeper:

> Widowed, infected, illiterate, and impoverished, Marianna sought a more humane life for her child in the sanctuary of the West. The sanctuary is heavily guarded, of course; from the outside, it looks more like a fortress, with high-tech, weaponized ramparts. Every day thousands throw themselves at its walls in leaky boats that wash up on the beaches of the Mediterranean, or by trekking through the American desert, or by boarding airplanes with vague dreams and papers that will be contemptuously scrutinized – dreams and papers both.[3]

It is, or was, also the architectural basis of many parts of Europe. One does not have to see the dead body of a child refugee, washed up on the shores of a Mediterranean coastline, to appreciate the stakes here. The walls are high, and grow higher by the day.

But that was then and this is now. The global pandemic of early 2020 was no respecter of borders – though its effects were felt disproportionately, as always, according to race and class. What then of community, and the very idea of inclusion? Before, the main problem was walls: some figurative (financial, cultural), some material (border fences, passport checkpoints). Now the problem of community becomes one where walls and border, indeed thresholds of all previous kinds, simply do not apply. Let us, then, consider the idea of community under these conditions – which are not so much *new* as more *vivid*, which is to say, more willing to limn the contours of reality.

Immunity

One's thoughts and memories turn, maybe unwillingly, to Thomas Robert Malthus's "principle of population." There is geometric increase in population, Malthus contentiously argued, but only linear increase in food. Hence there would be an inevitable eventual famine, or a resource scarcity of some other disastrous

COMMUNITYCOMMUNI
RISKRISKRISKRISKRI
JUSTICEJUSTICEJUSTI
AUTHORITARIANAUTH

WHAT IS COMMUNITY?

LIBERALLIBERALLIBER
POPULISTPOPULISTPO
INCLUSIONINCLUSIONI
EXCLUSIONEXCLUSION

kind. Malthus considered this a natural condition of limited ecospheres with rigid boundaries. Thus the need, he argued, for either drastic redistribution of resources, or else constantly renewed and expanded growth to relieve the pressure.[4] But there are going to be limits on the latter, and political objections to the former. Malthus ignores the possibility of expanding the limits of ecospheres, and makes his geometric-arithmetic logic unassailable. Those are clear conceptual errors. But he is perhaps correct that there are boundaries beyond which we cannot adapt, and he also implies by example that the politics of panic will be focused on control rather than cooperation.

Any situation of hard resource limit is bad enough, and arguably part of the pre-pandemic reality even when correcting for the lack of nuance in Malthus. Now suppose that you expand "food" to mean resources more generally, or indeed the entire biosphere. The issues return with renewed force. Malthus thought there would be demographic "corrections" when overcrowding and demand created crisis: famines, obviously, but also pestilence and disease; and, of course, war – now understood clearly as a conflict over control of land and associated resources. Ideology is in play here, as are motivating notions of honor and courage in battle, but mostly as window-dressing for basic depredation and conquest of desirable property. It is impossible to ignore the economics of war.

Then we arrive at our current moment, where "herd immunity" is another way of saying "vulnerable-demographic firebreak" on the spread of a virus under conditions of resource limits. This is the only viable alternative to a safe, early, and universally available vaccine, which remains the gold standard for overcoming any pandemic. The goal, said public health expert David Katz, "is natural herd immunity, achieved by those of us at low risk for severe infection, who can most safely go back to work and school and life as we knew it, while taking the right, reasonable protections. Meanwhile, we should guard those most vulnerable until we can sound the all-clear. Only this kind of thoughtful, risk-stratified approach can allow for herd immunity with maximal safety and minimal total harm from infection and the consequences of prolonged lockdown alike."[5]

With viruses such as this one, however, as much as 70% of the population might need to contract it in order to protect the overall herd. Suppose this can actually be done. The semi-palatable versions of the risk-stratification and the herd-immunity strategies typically then break into *natural* and *forced* options. The natural option is the scenario in which enough of a given population shows immunity to a virus to halt further spread. The forced option, which might include variolation (as with smallpox, where infected tissue becomes the basis of a vaccine) or volunteer infection, which singles out segments of the population for controlled infection and the resulting collection of antibodies. There is a third option, namely vaccination, to introduce overall immunity directly – albeit very slowly.

The brutal version of the thesis, by contrast, is this: we should simply open up the population to viral spread, especially if the effects of other, less radical measures include irreparable economic damage. Let the old, sick, and poor bear the brunt of the virus-based population "correction" so that the young, healthy, and wealthy can continue the human race.

If we attempt to limit the virus's spread with mitigating measures that distribute the risks across the entire population, the overall death tolls may be lower, but the cumulative costs of all kinds will be much higher. The firebreak metaphor is apt: we should allow deadwood to burn, or even burn some of it ourselves, in order to keep the forest fire from engulfing the entire landscape. Trying to reduce the fire's force by dousing it at the advance edge saves marginally more trees overall but causes other kinds of far-reaching damage to the environment.

We are, however, talking about people and not trees. The conversation about viral counter-measures and the timeline for "liberating" the economy is muddy because we are not simply brutal, even as we also feel long-term pressures that are scary. One idea of ethical response (flatten the curve, ride out the viral storm, keep economic curbs in place for a long time even if that is very costly) competes with another ethical theory—almost too nasty to speak about—whereby "selective" reopening of the economy is exchanged for a "reasonable" death toll.

Resources

We can solve the food problem if we manage, through innovation and better distribution (not to mention curbs on insane waste-rates in the so-called developed world) to match population growth with resource growth. There are untapped resources of sustainable nourishment in our oceans and fields. (Hint: beef is probably not on the long-term future menu.) But we know that many resources are non-renewable and non-expandable by definition, not just through mismanagement and poor distribution. These are goods that are, in economic parlance, private if not in fact positional: competitive, double-rival, and double-excludable resources where your use entails my suffering. This situation, in fact, represents the very pinnacle of private goods versus public ones.

The category of private-perhaps-positional goods right now includes health care, which has become a series of zero-sum games even under a public health system: my respirator is a respirator you can't have; so is my hospital bed, and the attention of my nurse or physician. We keep trying to parse health as a public good when the truth is that, at point of distribution, it is anything but.

Social fault lines are exposed by the virus, and can only yawn wider. This is so within societies: rich vs. poor on access to care, but also on access to online education, for example, or the ability to stay home and still pay the bills, bake our sourdough bread, and watch Netflix. It is a bad time to be black in America (when was it not?) and to be poor anywhere. But there are also emergent competitions between nations and regions. Governors of American states competing for respirators and testing reagents are small change compared to the affliction of the virus on areas already suffering hunger, lack of clean water, reliable access to medication, and so on. We have no idea how all the global inequality is going to be exacerbated by the pandemic.

Prediction

This is an essay about community and risk written at an especially risky time. Every trip to the grocery store, every walk down a street, is currently a minefield of contagion chance. The odds here are largely incalculable because, though we can enumerate infections and deaths, we cannot render a good bet on something that travels through the air.

But there are no good prophecies now, if there ever were. All the punditry in the world about what post-pandemic life will look like is just so much hot air, and, in contrast to earlier eras of augury, with few attendant risks to the pronouncers even as there might be great costs for economies and societies governed by bad bets. "Ancient augurs and prophets were in high-risk professions," the critic Mark Lilla wrote. "Many lost their lives when their predictions failed to materialize, either executed by sovereigns or pulled apart by mobs. We see a bloodless version of this reaction today in the public's declining confidence in both the news media and the government."[6]

Worse, he notes, are predictions—no more rational or trustworthy than the next—which hasten social costs. Thus his own decision, which I will echo here, not to predict or prophesy. "[T]he post-Covid future doesn't exist. It will exist only after we have made it. Religious prophecy is rational, on the assumption that the future is in the gods' hands, not ours. Believers can be confident that what the gods say through the oracles' mouth or inscribe in offal will come to pass, independent of our actions. But if we don't believe in such deities, we have no reason to ask what will happen to us. We should ask only what we want to happen, and how to make it happen, given the constraints of the moment."[7] Amen to that, whether in a religious sense or not.

Justice

We in the developed world have been living in a resource-rich fantasyland of apparent prosperity and taken-for-granted comfort. It is and always has been a house of cards, though defended as a fortress. Consider Malthus once again: environmental crisis is unpredictable, and so are its results. Even the thickest cocoons can be breached, and not all the dead are the poor. The contrastive claim is likewise true: not all the suffering will be borne by the reckless and feckless, the covidiots clustered on newly opened Florida beaches or gathering—at the dangerously incompetent president's urging— to protest "tyrannical" public-health measures in Minnesota, Virginia, and Michigan.

Humans are clever when it comes to their own self-preservation, but they can also be monumentally stupid. Perhaps unfortunately, Darwin's principle of natural selection only targets the dumb when measured over large numbers and

1 Mark Kingwell, *On Risk* (Biblioasis, 2020).

2 The comment was widely reported. See, for example, Marc Bennetts, "Western liberalism is obsolete, warns Putin, ahead of May meeting," *The Guardian* (June 28, 2019).

3 Ken Kalfus, *Coupe de Foudre: A Novella and Stories* (Bloomsbury, 2015), 52. Kalfus's story originally appeared in *Harper's Magazine* (April 2014).

4 See Thomas R. Malthus, *An Essay on the Principle of Population* (orig. 1798, expanded version 1803, Appendix 1806), Joyce E. Chaplin, ed. (W.W. Norton, 2017).

5 Quoted in Thomas L. Friedman, "Is Trump Trying to Spread Covid-19?" *New York Times* (June 16, 2020). "It is absolutely devilish," Friedman wrote, "like Trump wakes up every morning and asks himself: What health expert's advice can I defy today? What simple gesture to reduce the odds that the coronavirus continues to surge, post-lockdowns, can I ignore today? What quack remedy can I promote today?"

6 Mark Lilla, "No One Knows What's Going to Happen," *New York Times* (May 22, 2020).

7 Ibid.

8 Joseph-Achille Mbembé, "Necropolitics," Libby Meintjes, trans. *Public Culture* 15, no. 1 (Winter 2003): 11–40.

9 Jacques Derrida has written on hope— sometimes "hope beyond hope"—in a number of sources. A good introduction, which argues (contra Richard Rorty) that Derrida's notion of hopeless hope is socially utopian yet nevertheless politically effective is Mark Dooley, "Private irony vs. social hope: Derrida, Rorty, and the political," *Cultural Values* 3 (March 2009): 263–90.

10 See, for example, a working paper from the National Bureau of Economic Research, "Fatalism, Beliefs, and Behaviors During the COVID-19 Pandemic" (May 2020). The authors note that "individuals dramatically overestimate the infectiousness of COVID-19 relative to expert opinion" but that "providing people with expert information partially corrects their beliefs about the virus." And yet, "the more infectious people believe that COVID-19 is, the less willing they are to take social distancing measures, a finding we dub the 'fatalism effect.' We estimate that small changes in people's beliefs can generate billions of dollars in mortality benefits." This behavior will be familiar to anyone who witnessed the unfolding of the 2020 pandemic, but more to the larger point will recognize this as quintessential human activity. Soldiers, sailors, and sufferers of mortal disease are especially prone to such fatalism; but we are all its potential victims, whenever we abandon hope as we enter the gates of our personal hells.

11 Julian Brave NoiseCat, "How to Survive and Apocalypse and Keep Dreaming," *The Nation* (June 2, 2020). NoiseCat also relates Cowboy Smithx's plan to purchase Castle Calgary in Scotland and rename it *mohkinstsis*, which means "elbow" – the original Blackfoot name for Calgary, Alberta, where the Bow River bends. This is what Smithx labels "inverted colonialism."

spans of time. In the short term, wealthy dummies have a better chance of survival than even the most intelligent members of vulnerable subpopulations.

The essential question of all human societies has ever been this: Who will live and who will die? This is what the philosopher Achille Mbembé expressed in the following stark language in a 2003 essay called "Necropolitics": "The ultimate expression of sovereignty resides, to a large degree, in the power and capacity to dictate who may live and who must die. Hence, to kill or allow to live constitutes the limits of sovereignty, its fundamental attributes."[8] *That* is what sovereignty really means, friends – and it is not Malthusian in the negative sense to acknowledge it. And yet, the existential baseline drawn beneath those calculations remains of course John Maynard Keynes's ultimate socio-economic conclusion: "In the long run, we are all dead." True enough (and, for Keynes, more about monetary policy than life philosophy); but in the present, we need to be thinking hard about when, why, and how many are dead, not just lurching from reaction to reaction. The virus is neither brutal nor just; it simply is. What it portends and achieves is up to us.

Justice does not mean a return to the dark dream of pre-pandemic normal. That is not in the interests of community. Justice starts, at least, with a recognition that the normal was deeply and inherently unjust. There were already population firebreaks before the pandemic, brutal mechanisms of immunity constructed of barbed wire fencing and birthright exclusion. New firebreaks of the reckless and stupid are not defensible in current discourse, which is a victory for decency but maybe a defeat for global equity. Meanwhile, we lurch on into our near future, caught between the dilemmatic horns of mass death and economic collapse. Is there any resolution here? We must hope so, but whatever it is will not, and should not, mean a return to what went before. The risks there are only too obvious.

And so now, let us move on to the next staging-ground of contingency. Or, as a solider would say, we now have to advance in defilade and watch for flanking fire – otherwise known as emergent unforeseen risks, the kind that cut us down in enfilade. These military metaphors usually strike me as unseemly, if not actively harmful; but right now it feels as if the world is on a kind of war footing and we need to think in tactical and strategic terms.

Community

So what *is* community as we head into the third decade of the 21st century? It is a morass of confusion and contradiction, to be sure, but also still a beacon of hope for a world in which we accommodate not just the robust trees but also the most vulnerable and at-risk ones.

This last idea is, after all, the governing norm of the past centuries of nation-building, global connection, and international law.

We have grown, by difficult stages, more and more inclusive. And, while pockets and even systems of exclusion obviously remain–wealth inequality, racial and gender intolerance, colonial and environmental depredation–there is always room left over for hope: what the French philosopher Jacques Derrida memorably defined as "the unresolved remainder" when all daily dialectic had done its sublating work.[9]

That remainder, the undigested bit of human reason that somehow lies beyond reason, is our best chance for future community. It is distinct from optimism, which many experts warned us, in the first months of pandemic lockdown, could be a recipe for anxiety, depression, or bad predictions. Optimism is keyed to the idea of a return to normal, without questioning the darkness of the dreams that dominate that state of affairs from a time before – what a Latin-trained writer would call the *status quo ante*.

Optimism is also dangerous if it impairs more existentially inflected forms of coping, because it becomes easy prey to disappointment, and hence a dangerous fatalism.[10] But then optimism and pessimism become almost indistinguishable judgments on the glass containing half its volume: Half-full? Half-empty? *Same thing*. Returning to Leibnizian theodicy for a moment, the philosophical old joke has it that the optimist believes he is living in the best of all possible worlds. The pessimist fears that this is true.

And, finally, to continue with yet another military analogy, surviving prisoners of war sometimes describe how those without optimism had a better chance of retaining sanity amidst insanity. They did not expect any kind of return; and that made them especially resilient to the daily insults and terrors of imprisonment.

As I was pondering various responses to risks and consequences during the pandemic-dominated weeks of this writing, I came across an article that felt unlike all the other things I had been reading, both contemporary and historical. It was by the writer Julian Brave NoiseCat, of the Secwepemc/St'at'imc First Nations, called in English the Interior Squalish people and based in the Central and Southern Interior regions of British Columbia, near towns like Kamloops, Chase, D'Arcy, and Lillooet. The essay related how he heard the Blackfoot filmmaker Cowboy Smithx, from Southern Alberta, describe Native culture as one of "post-apocalyptic people."

What he meant, NoiseCat suggested, was something like this: "As Indians, I think we've been told that we're supposed to be dead and gone so many times that we've internalized it. Some of us don't want to be anymore. In a society built atop our graves, survival has become an act of resistance." And further, it meant this: "We've inherited a vision so audacious, it terrified our oppressors. It's a worldview that celebrates beauty, defiance, and a playful wagging of the finger at the people who tried to kill us. After the pandemic but as the climate crisis unfolds, maybe more people will understand what it means to survive and still dream, like us."[11]

The last comment followed hard on details of how L. Frank Baum, beloved creator of *The Wonderful Wizard of Oz* (1900), had written an editorial in the *Aberdeen Saturday Pioneer*, a week after the December 29, 1890, massacre and mass burial of Lakota ghost dancers by the United States military. The editorial included this genocidal injunction: "Our only safety depends upon the total extermination of the Indians. Having wronged them for centuries we had better, in order to protect our civilization, follow it up by one more wrong and wipe these untamed and untamable creatures from the face of the earth." Which is the kind of double-down logic all too common in our own day, 130 years later.

What is it to be "post-apocalyptic"? Well, it is not to entertain the usual play of utopian and dystopian options so often found in speculative fiction and CGI-heavy films, illuminating or entertaining though those may be. Too often, that binary division in imaginative rendering of life after apocalypse collapses into a futile and meaningless simulacrum of dialectic thought – usually executed with lots of expensive cinematic special effects. Rather, to be post-apocalyptic is to contemplate the total destruction of one's culture *even when* one's life continues. And then it is to witness, without apology and often with hypocritical "antiracist" virtue-signaling, the names and images of that culture repurposed as sports logos, gas-station signs, or trade names for butter and syrup.[12]

To survive and still to dream. This is to imagine beyond optimism, to transcend possibility and probability both, after the manner of what Jonathan Lear, writing of the destruction of the American Crow people, called "radical hope."[13] Like most people of privilege and comfort, living in my corner of the house of cards, I don't really know what that feels like. But I try to make sense of it, as we watch the world turned on its head, becoming a warren of risk and attendant injustices. I want, like so many of us, to believe in an audacious vision. But maybe we have to survive apocalypse before we can even dream that transcendent dream.

We are not yet prisoners of war, just of circumstance; we are not yet victims of military massacre, though the prospect is continually held in reserve, at the ready. We want to be survivors, but only if we can be together. Hope limns the contours of community, now and always. Bet on that, friends. It really is our only play

12 In the immediate wake of anti-Black racism protests over the killing of George Floyd by police, celebrities and corporations rushed to embrace the suddenly acceptable, even trendy, position of protest. The resulting Twitter meme known as "This you?" mocked these self-serving half- or quarter-measures by lining up past racists acts, campaigns, or features of the would-be social justice warriors.

13 Jonathan Lear, *Radical Hope: Ethics in the Face of Cultural Devastation* (Harvard University Press, 2008). In this book Lear concentrates on Plenty Coups, the last great Chief of the Crow Nation, who related to the white philosopher the story of his people – up to a certain point. "When the buffalo went away the hearts of my people fell to the ground," he said, "and they could not lift them up again. After this nothing happened." This notion of nothing happened is central to the radical nature of hope: normal events are suspended; there are no events; time is stopped or simply over. And yet life, or at least survival, goes on.

Garrett Dash Nelson is the Curator of Maps and Director of Geographic Scholarship at the Leventhal Map & Education Center at the Boston Public Library. He works in the disciplines of historical geography, landscape studies, and critical cartography to understand the relationship between the definition of places, the organization of community life, and the politics of planning.

+ GEOGRAPHY, SOCIOLOGY, PLANNING

One of the great difficulties with the term "community" is that its meaning is confusingly perched between sociology and geography. A community is sometimes a group, at other times a place, and most often some tricky hybrid in which a group and a place constitute one another.

On the one hand, the simplest definition of community is a group of people bound together by some common interest. While this sociological definition of community is theoretically flexible enough to apply to nearly any set of people of any kind, in practice it most frequently refers to a group that is small in number and whose common features are deep and interpenetrating enough to support forms of mutual recognition. In this sense, the community is the next-largest social circle above the kin or family group. This definition makes the community a group of people who know each other well and who can generate some organic kind of common feeling due to the fact that their common interest exceeds a mere coincidental attachment – thus, a group of people who have lived and labored together for many years form a community in the way that, say, a group of people who happen to be passengers on the same airplane do not. This bias against groups that are linked together by mechanistic and formal attributes is inherited from one of the concept's original theorists, Ferdinand Tönnies, who proposed a dichotomy between *Gemeinschaft* (almost always translated as community) and *Gesellschaft* (more ambiguously translated as society, or, sometimes, economy).[1] From Tönnies onward, sociological descriptions of community have very often injected the term with connotations of naturalism, authenticity, voluntarism, and affection.

On the other hand, though sometimes in the very same invocation, a community is also a place, a specifically identifiable patch of the Earth's surface. As with its sociological meaning, the geographic definition of a community also has a subtle but strong bias toward smallness and locality; the nearest synonym is neighborhood, or—once again suggesting the premodern connotation

ON THE EDGES OF COMMUNITY

GARRETT DASH NELSON

Previous: "Teeter-Totter Wall," an installation at
the US-Mexico border wall by architecture studio
Rael San Fratello, brings communities from both
countries together in play.

which haunts the term–village. Though conceptually distinct, the sociological and geographic definitions of community are hardly without correlation, for a basic reciprocity between propinquity and group life links the two together. The meaningful, long-duration interpersonal relationships that are the invisible filaments of the sociological community are easiest to weave amongst people who live close together, and so geographic neighbors are some of the first candidates for inclusion into a social community. In the reverse direction, geographic communities are never just arbitrary geometries drawn on a map, but places that are imbued with the historical and morphological specificity of a human group's presence.

This reciprocity between social commonality and geographic location is certainly not an unambiguous one-to-one relationship, for there are countless examples where mere proximate neighborliness has not been enough to form meaningful social ties between people riven apart by other identities like race, ethnicity, and class. Yet they are closely enough linked that even the precise *Oxford English Dictionary* elides them together: "A body of people who live in the same place, usually sharing a common cultural or ethnic identity. Hence: a place where a particular body of people lives."[2] The rather astonishing causal leap accomplished by the word "hence" in this definition indicates just how semantically effortless it can be to jump from social commonality to geographic location.

The two distinct meanings become apparent again, however, when faced with the question of how to define what is *in* a community and what is *out*, both in a conceptual and practical sense. Do we enter a community simply by stepping inside its geographic borders or do we only enter it when we are absorbed into its social matrix? Is the edge of a community a line on the ground, suitable for tracing on a map, or is it the metaphorical line of a Venn diagram's circle, inside which lie the people with some social attribute in common but whose real-world geometry is impossible to draw? If we seek the counsel of the community for, say, a new park project, who are we asking? Anybody who lives nearby? Anybody who lives within the boundaries of some predefined subdivision of a city or jurisdiction? Or, are we asking a group defined by its characteristics, like "the immigrant community" or "the LGBTQ community"? As a young Lewis Mumford, observing the complicated functional interdependence of cities and regions, jotted down in a note from the early 1920s: "The crux of the difficulty is the unit of investigation. What is a society or a community?"[3]

Closely attached to this question of who is in and who is out of a community is a question of how extensible–both spatially and categorically–the term might be. Due to its assumed predisposition toward the small and the local, the community is very often cast as the opposite or counterpoint position to something that is large, abstract, or formally structured. Practices such as "community participation" or "community-driven design" are meant to bring the supposed wisdom and site-specific knowledge of ordinary people to bear on processes that otherwise would be driven by experts and élites. Here the "community" explicitly functions as the counterposition of and the counterweight to such organizations as the government, the state, or the corporation, a typical reinscription of the *Gemeinschaft–Gesellschaft* divide.

But what makes the rather vaguely defined "ordinary people" a meaningful community in a way that other groups are not? Surely, state bureaucrats, with their close educational and professional networks, a shared specialized vocabulary, and very often affective bonds that exceed the functional necessities of their work, also form a kind of community. And, similarly, why must the community, invoked in this manner, perform a kind of magical consubstantiation with smallness and locality? When deciding whether or not to desegregate a school, for instance, is the community who has the highest right to intervene on this question a small, organically constituted set of a few hundred families attending the school, or is the proper community in this case some far-larger set of people, perhaps even the universal set of all humans invoked in principles of human rights?

The trouble that lies at the shunting-point of the various meanings of community is particularly salient for those who work to design landscapes, because they are charged (or ought to be charged) with a twin social and geographical mandate. After all, the very word landscape expresses the same duality as community, albeit in a manner that has been gradually scrubbed out of the English language: the early Germanic word *Landschaft*, from which our modern English term landscape is descended, referred to a relatively self-governing polity whose distinctness was formed over time by "the combination of community, custom, and territory," as the geographer Denis Cosgrove writes.[4] Community and landscape are therefore joined together at their semantic origin point, for both describe the connective tissue through which group social life and the distinct identity of places are constitutive of one another. Either tacitly or explicitly, this reciprocity is widely recognized by landscape architects, as in Garrett Eckbo's observation that "the thinking on park design and on urbanism and community planning will move toward a merger," such that "the park space will become the functional skeleton of the community, and this articulated, clarified, chlorophylled, and sunlighted community will find it finally possible to enter into communal relations with the landscape of the site."[5]

It is precisely the power of a landscape to give shape to a community's sense of self that has motivated many designers

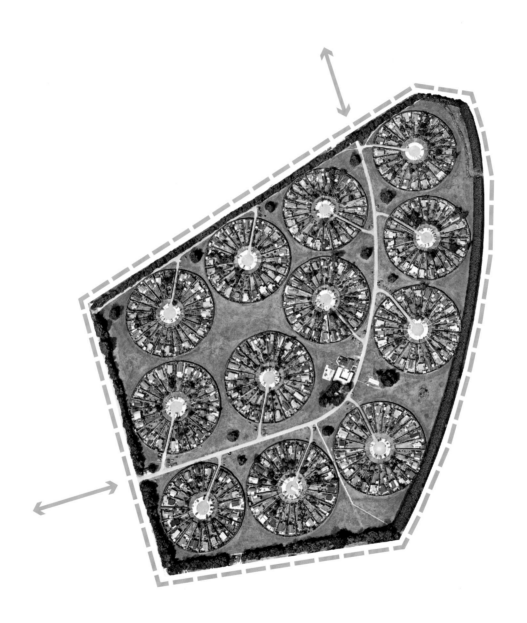

and critics from the 19th century onward to pay great attention to the role of *edges* in the built environment. Because landscape and community shade into one another, each alternatively serving as a signifier of the other, a well-structured landscape, with a distinct form of centers and edges, seems to form the identifying parameters–the "functional skeleton," to borrow Eckbo's words–of a coherent community. Meanwhile, a profound fear of this ideal's antithesis–the sprawling, edgeless, formless, indiscrete, atomized landscape–is ever-present in the intellectual history of landscape architecture and planning. Benton MacKaye described this ideal/antithesis in an instructive set of binaries, which he brought to bear on a scathing critique of the industrial metropolis. The sprawling motor city's built environment, MacKaye complained, "is intrusive, not innate; it is a massing, not a unit, a collection not a community, an inorganic deposit not an organism."[6]

The specter of the intrusive-massing-collection-deposit landscape has continued to frighten designers both before and as-group, makes it appear that the social community also dissipates and fractures within such landscapes. As the geographer David Matless writes about the design ideology that emerged in interwar England:

> Ideals of community and landscape were often defined in relation to what might be termed "anti-community," modes of settlement and conduct labelled by critics as socially and scenically inappropriate, and whose presence challenged or undermined visions of planned and progressive (or indeed traditionalist and reactionary) order.[7]

British planners like Patrick Abercrombie and Clough Williams-Ellis came to sanctify the well-edged premodern parish as the supreme example of a coextensive landscape and community at just the same time that Americans like MacKaye and Mumford were elevating the New England township to a similarly venerated status. It is important to note that this celebration did not necessarily translate into strictly traditionalist aesthetic templates, but, instead, formed a deep conceptual crossing-point between landscape and the prototypically "organic" forms of community, which could then be abstracted into modern idioms. The arch-modernist Walter Gropius, for instance, in a 1945 lecture, critiqued the "true symbol of disunity" formed by a sprawling industrial metropolis, one which marked a "disrupted and decayed community life" and counterpoised it to the "well-balanced, self-imposed order and unity," which characterized the New England town and the "spirit of its community."[8]

It was a landscape architect, Henry Wright, who was one of the first to combine the terms "community" and "planning" to argue for a form of landscape intervention oriented toward the community as both a social ideal and morphological form. By designing intentionally for groups and clusters of homes and related service centers, Wright argued, it would become possible to "compose a well ordered community."[9] Marjorie L. Sewell Cautley, who worked with Wright on the designs for Radburn and Sunnyside, was similarly sensitive to the role of landscape design as the context in which functional community ties would take place. As the landscape historian Thaïsa Way writes, Cautley designed "articulated spaces, visually accessible landscapes, and identifiable circulation patterns" with the aim of giving residents the physical spaces in which they could recognize, meet, and interact with one another and thereby knit together the mutualistic social relations on which a genuine community might be built.

Both the theoretical and formal twin of the distinctly edged landscape was the centered landscape: an open area that could serve as a focal point for community life. Here again, a powerful semantic tradition was at play, for the *commons* of the premodern parish or village was both etymologically and functionally inseparable from the life of the *community* that gathered around it. MacKaye, writing about his hometown of Shirley, Massachusetts, wrote "As the nucleus of the community setting is the plot of land known as '*The* Common' so the focus of the community spirit is the mind and purpose we have '*in* common.'"[10] In arguments such as these, the binding together of community-as-place and community-as-group once again becomes evident. The commons should not be interpreted as the *post hoc* creation of some already-existent community; to the contrary, the commons, as a focal landscape around which people organize their lives, *creates* the community itself.

The attempt to create a legible edge and center in the landscape for a community *as a place* so that it will form a conceptual whole for the community *as a group of people* is a highly contestable project, however, due its ability to serve strikingly different political ideologies. The totemic power of Donald Trump's border wall in charging a potent new strain of ethnonational chauvinism is only the most recent example of a long history of using geographic edges to define an exclusionary form of community belonging. At a smaller geographic scale, gated or racially restricted neighborhoods may well promote a sense of bound-together community within their strictly defined borders, but invidious, negatively defined communities such as these should never be the ones that a progressive design seeks to create.

Catherine Bauer Wurster, both an ally and prescient critic of Mumford and MacKaye, realized this difficulty when she noted in 1945 that "the image brought to mind by the word

'neighborhood' or 'community' is likely still to be that of a small New England eighteenth-century town." Yet, as Bauer noted, once the real economic and social conditions that had supported the premodern village had vanished, what typically remained when modern planners anachronistically fetishized the community was a "feudal idea of subdividing the city map into a series of standardized watertight compartments."[11] As Bauer realized, the linking together of a community as a discrete place and community as an idealized form of social life could run in both progressive and reactionary directions, for the dark twin of solidarity is segregation. Such an ambiguity is evident in the complicated work of the architect Ralph Adams Cram, who was both a critic of capitalist modernity as well as a deeply religious believer, and whose 1920 book *Walled Towns* presented an ideologically complicated version of the landscape-and-community principle, in which the community is both traditional and radical, distinctly marked into an organic unity that points simultaneously at both communism and conservatism.[12]

What is the landscape architect's responsibility, then, to the ideal of community as both a place and social group, and how does that ideal take form through its edges and centers? Perhaps one solution is to treat the edge of a community as both boundary *and* meeting place, thereby muddling the conceptual distinction between center and edge. An interesting metaphor can be found in an argument made by Andrew Haswell Green, the influential 19th-century park administrator, in favor of the political consolidation of New York City's boroughs. Looking at the rivers that formed the edge landscapes between Manhattan, Brooklyn, and the other municipalities that were then debating union, Green wrote "it is perversion of thought and policy to regard these bonds of union as symbols of division, and to find in the paths by which we are united the lines by which we are all separated."[13] As Green put it, the edge between one community and another was also the conduit by which those communities were intimately linked to one another: the border was also a gateway.

If the physical edges of community-as-place are simultaneously linkages outward, then, similarly, the conceptual edges of community-as-group must be softened to recognize the essential role of outward interdependence and interconnection to the life of even the smallest, most tightly defined social community. It is possible to give form and structure to the geography of a community without strangling it inside a deluded vision of autonomy and autarky, just as it is possible for a community to recognize the reality of its mutual life without rejecting its dependence on other communities, both those that intersect it and those that neighbor it.

1 Ferdinand Tönnies, *Community and Society (Gemeinschaft Und Gesellschaft)*, trans. Charles P. Loomis (Harper & Row, 1963); see also Louis Wirth, "The Sociology of Ferdinand Tönnies," *American Journal of Sociology* 32, no. 3 (1926): 412–22.

2 Oxford English Dictionary, "community, n.," *OED Online*, oed.com/view/Entry/37337.

3 Lewis Mumford Papers, University of Pennsylvania Kislak Center, 188:8168.

4 Denis Cosgrove, "Landscape and Landschaft," *GHI Bulletin* 35 (2004): 61; see also Kenneth Olwig, *Landscape, Nature, and the Body Politic: From Britain's Renaissance to America's New World* (University of Wisconsin Press, 2002); Kenneth Olwig, "Recovering the Substantive Nature of Landscape" *Annals of the Association of American Geographers* 86, no. 4 (1996): 630–53; J.B. Jackson, "The Meanings of 'Landscape,'" *Kulturgeografi* 16, no. 88 (1964): 1614–18.

5 Garrett Eckbo, *Landscape for Living* (University of Massachusetts Press, 2009), 44.

6 Benton MacKaye, "End or Peak of Civilization?" *Survey Graphic* 21, no. 7 (1932): 444.

7 David Matless, "Communities of Landscape: Nation, Locality, and Modernity in Interwar England," in Rajesh Heynickx & Tom Avermaete (eds), *Making a New World: Architecture & Communities in Interwar Europe* (Leuven University Press, 2012), 43.

8 "Rebuilding our Communities After the War: A talk given by Dr. Walter Gropius, Chairman of the Graduate School of Architecture, Harvard University, on Friday, February 23, 1945, at the Palmer House," Walter Gropius Papers, Harvard University Houghton Library, folder 75.

9 Henry Wright, "Shall We Community Plan?" *Journal of the American Institute of Architects* 9, no. 10 (1921): 323.

10 Benton MacKaye, "What the Tercentenary Celebration Can Mean to the Montachusett Region," (ca. 1929), MacKaye Family Papers, Dartmouth College Rauner Library, 178: 7.

11 Catherine Bauer, "Good Neighborhoods," *Annals of the American Academy of Political and Social Science* 242 (1945): 104–15.

12 Ralph Adams Cram, *Walled Towns* (Marshall Jones Company, 1920).

13 Andrew Haswell Green, *New York of the Future: Writings and Addresses by Andrew H. Green* (1893), 14.

THE INTERCULTURAL

CONTACT, DISTANCE, SPACE, AND PLACE

CITY

6'

6'

JULIAN AGYEMAN

Julian Agyeman is a professor and critical urban planning scholar at Tufts University in the United States. He is the originator of the increasingly influential concept of just sustainabilities: the intentional integration of social justice and sustainability. His research centers on critical explorations of the complex and embodied relations between humans and the urban environment, whether mediated by governments or social movement organizations, and their effects on public policy and planning processes and outcomes, particularly in relation to notions of justice and equity.

+ URBAN PLANNING

Public spaces are simultaneously symbols of government, religion, culture, and economy. Communities around the world continue to fight for, create, and recreate public spaces. From pocket parks to PARK(ing) Day, they are carved from the commerce of urban centers, the interstitial spaces and abandoned industrial structures of yesteryear, and even automobile-lined streets. These spaces are part of the intimacy of the city. They are used for everything from people-watching to protests and political revolutions. But all that changed in 2020 as COVID-19 rewrote the rules about our lives in public spaces, neighborhoods, streets, even whole cities themselves.

Social or Physical Distancing?

The new code of public space is *social distancing*. It has become the phrase *du jour* as governments worldwide encourage people to work from home and to avoid gathering in any form of urban space. But is this what we really want or need? Isn't *physical distancing* a better phrase? It conveys the same essential public health message, but avoids the social distancing—or worse social isolation—which contributes to our growing fear and anxiety, especially our fear of "the other." Socially, more than ever, don't we need to come together?

And this is happening. In Canada, driven by social media, the altruism of *caremongering* has taken hold and it is spreading. It is characterized by acts of kindness, to stop anxiety, isolation, and lack of hope. Typical acts include checking in, going to the supermarket for those who are unable, or offering to cook meals. In mid-March, over 35 Facebook groups appeared in a 72-hour period to help communities in Ottawa, Halifax, and Annapolis County, Nova Scotia with over 30,000 members in total. In Toronto what was an idea among a few concerned residents grew to over 9,000 members. Similarly, in the US, communities are reaching out to those in need to pick up groceries, cities are using school buses to deliver free meals, and local chefs are turning restaurants into community kitchens. It seems that altruism and kindness may be as contagious as coronavirus.

So how do we grow this natural human tendency toward altruism?[1] How do we reinforce and deepen the concept of the civic realm, of public space in a time of COVID-19, and after? How do we practice physical distancing without social isolation and segregation? And how do we develop *spaces of encounter*: spaces that encourage contact with "the other," across social and cultural difference?

Contact Theory

Let's start with Contact Theory which posits that intergroup contact, under certain circumstances, reduces prejudice between majority and minority groups.[2] Today, many of us live in *cities of difference*[3] – namely, our increasingly different, diverse, and culturally heterogeneous urban areas. These are places where we are in *the presence of otherness*.[4] Following Patsy Healey's charge that urban planning is about "managing our co-existence in shared space,"[5] a focus of our work should be both creating and encouraging the use of public spaces as places of contact, mixing, engagement, and encounter across difference to help decrease social distancing, isolation, and segregation. Jeffrey Hou asks, "How can urban places function as vehicles for cross-cultural learning and understanding rather than just battlegrounds and turfs?"[6] Elijah Anderson calls these spaces "cosmopolitan canopies"; for example, Reading Terminal Market, Philadelphia, where cross-cultural and cross-racial civility occurs.[7] Others have noted that, "interracial interactions that occur in leisure settings (e.g., parks and public spaces) have the potential to be more genuine compared with the more obligatory interactions that take place in formal (e.g., workplace) settings."[8] In sum, interactions between members of different groups can reduce intergroup prejudice under the right conditions.[9] An understanding of the possibilities, and limitations of Contact Theory should be central to an urban planning and design education.

However, Contact Theory offers little or no guidance on *how* to achieve culturally inclusive space, let alone how to achieve such spaces in places where social inequality is deeply entrenched.[10] Additionally, contact with diverse groups may serve to make shifts in personal prejudice, but it has been shown to have little impact on structural discrimination[11], such as biased policing methods, which may have a much greater impact on a particular group's spatial practices and use of public space.[12]

It's not easy. Designing inclusive public space faces many obstacles and challenges, especially when trying to engage with difference, diversity, and cultural heterogeneity in creative and productive ways. Anastasia Loukaitou-Sideris argues that many public areas have, "reinforced divisions based upon class, race, age, or ethnicity."[13] Setha Low et al. are even more forthright: "In this new century, we are facing a different kind of threat to public space—not one of disuse, but of patterns of design and management that exclude some people and reduce social and cultural diversity."[14]

I argue it is possible to plan, design, and maintain *culturally inclusive spaces* or at the very least minimize *culturally exclusive spaces*, but this necessitates, among other things, a paradigm shift in our thinking from multiculturalism to interculturalism and the prioritization of cultural literacy and competency, to move us toward *culturally inclusive practice.*

1 Matt Ridley, *The Origins of Virtue* (Viking, 1996).

2 Gordon Allport, *The Nature of Prejudice* (Perseus Books, 1954).

3 Ruth Fincher & Jane Jacobs, *Cities of Difference* (Guilford Press, 1998).

4 Richard Sennett, *The Conscience of the Eye: The design and social life of cities* (Knopf, 1990).

5 Patsy Healy, *Collaborative Planning – Shaping Places in Fragmented Societies* (UBC Press, 1997), 3.

6 Jeffrey Hou, *Transcultural Cities: Border-Crossing and Placemaking* (Routledge, 2013), 1.

7 Elijah Anderson, *The Cosmopolitan Canopy: Race and Civility in Everyday Life* (W. W. Norton & Company, 2011).

8 Kimberly Shinew, Troy Glover & Diana Parry, "Leisure Spaces as Potential Sites for Interracial Interaction: Community Gardens in Urban Areas," *Journal of Leisure Research* 36, no. 3 (2004): 338.

9 John Dixon, Kevin Durrheim & Colin Tredoux, "Beyond the Optimal Contact Strategy: A reality check for the contact hypothesis," American Psychologist 60, no. 7 (2005); Emily Talen, *Design for Diversity: Exploring Socially Mixed Neighborhoods* (Architectural Press, 2008).

10 Dixon, et al., ibid.

11 Ibid.

12 Myron Floyd, James Gramann & Rogelio Saenz, "Ethnic Factors and the Use of Public Outdoor Recreation Areas: The case of Mexican Americans," *Leisure Sciences* 15, no. 2 (1993): 83–98; Margaret Arnold & Kimberly Shinew, "The Role of Gender, Race, and Income on Park Use Constraints" *Journal of Park and Recreation Administration* 16, no. 4 (1998).

13 Anastasia Loukaitou-Sideris, "Children's Common Grounds: A Study of Intergroup Relations Among Children in Public Settings," *Journal of the American Planning Association* 69, no. 2 (2003): 131.

14 Setha Low, Dana Taplin & Suzanne Scheld, *Rethinking Urban Parks Public Space and Cultural Diversity* (University of Texas Press, 2005), 1.

15 James Tully, *Strange Multiplicity: Constitutionalism in an Age of Diversity* (Cambridge University Press, 1995).

16 Ash Amin, "Ethnicity and the Multicultural City: Living with Diversity," *Environment and Planning* (2016): 960.

17 Ibid.

18 Jude Bloomfield & Franco Bianchini, *Planning for the Cosmopolitan City: A research report for Birmingham City Council* (International Cultural Planning and Policy Unit, 2002): 6.

19 Leonie Sandercock, *Cosmopolis II: Mongrel Cities of the 21st Century* (Bloomsbury, 2003), 207–08.

Interculturalism

Multiculturalist discourses have fallen short in considering the broader impacts of culture on planning and sustainability. James Tully notes that multiculturalism, as it has been conceived, does not require any fundamental change in thinking; our societies, he argues, are intercultural rather than multicultural because of the cross-cultural overlap, interaction, and negotiation—the "politics of recognition"—that occur out of necessity in the formation of our society.[15] This is what Ash Amin calls the "negotiation of difference within local micro-publics of everyday interaction."[16] An acknowledgment of this dynamic cultural nature of society—both the politics of recognition and negotiation of difference—is a key distinction between intercultural and multicultural theory, demanding a culturally competent and inclusive approach to both planning and policymaking.[17]

Jude Bloomfield and Franco Bianchini make perhaps the most eloquent argument for interculturalism, the full implications of which should be fully understood by politicians, planners, urban designers, and policy makers:

> The interculturalism approach goes beyond opportunities and respect for existing cultural differences, to the pluralist transformation of public space, civic culture and institutions... city governments should promote cross-fertilisation across all cultural boundaries, between "majority" and "minorities", "dominant" and "sub" cultures, localities, classes, faiths, disciplines and genres, as the source of cultural, social, political and economic innovation.[18]

Leonie Sandercock, however, appeals to our emotions: "I dream of a city of bread and festivals, where those who don't have the bread aren't excluded from the carnival. I dream of a city in which action grows out of knowledge and understanding."[19] This city, Sandercock explains, would value social justice over balanced budgets, neighborhood discussion before decisions, and its very possibility should seduce us.

Imagine, for a moment, a mayor or city leadership group who had the courage to move in these directions, to contaminate and hybridize across cultures, to feel seduced by the city; a mayor or leadership group that refused to go with the status quo, with what is probable, but instead focused on what is possible. The transformation of Broadway and the High Line in New York City under Mayor Bloomberg are small but highly significant examples of possibility, as was the more ambitious development and implementation of London's Congestion Charge under Mayor Livingstone, or the "Copenhagen Miracle" under a succession of mayors since the 1960s and the guidance of the iconic urbanist Jan Gehl. However, the only citywide, culture-shifting examples that even come close to intercultural urban planning are the double act of Antanas Mockus and Enrique Peñalosa who literally performed (in the case of Mockus) the most celebrated of urban transformations in Bogotá, Colombia in the 1990s, and more recently the social urbanism-inspired transformation of Medellín, Colombia since the early 1980s.

Designing, Planning & Maintaining Culturally Inclusive Spaces

The uneven development and quality of public spaces across city neighborhoods is a classic case of spatial injustice. Most public spaces serve as meeting places for people who already know each other, and many open spaces are sites of tension and racism that reinforce intergroup separation.[20] Certain subgroups express additional difference-based barriers that concern language, disabilities, gender identity, and religion.

Despite these conceptual challenges, public spaces can be sites of huge intercultural opportunity. They may be the only sites where various groups interact at all, and organized events such as soccer matches, festivals, or youth group activities may offer important opportunities for intergroup contact[21] and for generating shared experiences.[22] People who have emigrated from one country and culture to another tend to use public open spaces and parks to gather and congregate in ways that are reminiscent of their home country, transforming the parks of their adoptive community into familiar spaces. People grow attached to spaces, to their aromas, textures, and the overall "feel" of a space.

Ashley Graves Lanfer and Madeline Taylor write about Latino immigrants in Boston, Massachusetts, who transform public spaces into familiar landscapes found in the group's home countries.[23] They have adopted Herter Park on the River Charles in Boston's Allston-Brighton neighborhood because it reminds them of the riverbanks and willow trees they left behind in Guatemala. Vacant lots, especially in Boston's Brighton neighborhood, have been transformed into squares reminiscent of Latin American plazas. Nicholas Dines and colleagues found that first-generation Asians in Newham, East London, UK, described feeling most comfortable in specific shopping corridors where there were fewer language barriers, as well as direct reminders of their countries of origin, such as foods and music.[24] In the context of the challenges associated with establishing oneself in a new place, these familiar-looking, familiar-sounding, familiar-smelling places enable the transfer of comforting cultural patterns from people's home landscapes to their new landscape.

How, then, do we get to Bloomfield and Bianchini's intercultural dream where "different cultures intersect, 'contaminate' each other and hybridize?"[25] Clearly, parks and public spaces have a role to play. Unfortunately, culturally inclusive spaces–those designed intentionally around the recognition of difference, diversity, and cultural heterogeneity–have not been a major focus of study in the planning literature, nor are they well understood by practicing urban designers, planners, and policymakers.[26]

When planning and (re)designing inclusive spaces, it is useful to refer to Julie Guthman's question, which is not "Who is *at* the table?" but "Who is *setting* the table?"[27] This is the first principle of culturally inclusive practice. It is critically important to draw from different cultures and subcultures and to include a variety of user-derived options. It is also important to focus efforts aimed at designing inclusive spaces on places that accommodate meaningful interaction among users, rather than simply on areas with the greatest number of people crossing paths.[28]

Ali Madanipour cautions: "If public spaces are produced and managed by narrow interests, they are bound to become exclusive places."[29] Therefore, the planning process must be inclusive. Planners are advised to forget about the monolithic "public" or the "average" user, and instead begin the open space planning process with "deep knowledge" of the preferences of the actual communities who are likely to use those spaces.[30] Clare Rishbeth et al. go further, noting that "data from ethnographic research can be of high value in refining questions, shaping priorities, and sometimes informing the detail, of urban design practice."[31] However, Yasminah Beebejaun warns against the dangers of determinism: "complexities exist both within and between cultures. One issue for planning in culturally diverse contexts is that different cultures, subcultures, and generations have different assumptions and conventions about who uses public space."[32]

Generating deep knowledge should involve ethnographic research as Rishbeth et al. suggest, coproduced by and with the communities concerned, to learn about the cultural backgrounds, perceptions, and needs of those in the local community regarding open space use. Equally important is an understanding of how users' past experiences in public spaces have shaped their use of or aspirations for the space now and in the future.[33] Fred Kent and others believe the best ideas for the future come from the community, and they should be actively engaged in creating public spaces at every stage of the process.[34]

Following good design principles is fundamental in creating high-quality open space but not sufficient in ensuring inclusivity.[35] A culturally inclusive space should offer amenities, rules, and landscapes that accommodate people of all ages and

20 Nicholas Dines, et al., *Public Spaces and Social Relations in East London* (Joseph Rowntree Foundation, 2006).

21 Ibid.

22 Hannah Lownsbrough & Joost Beunderman, *Equally Spaced? Public Space and Interaction between Diverse Communities: A Report for the Commission for Racial Equality* (Demos, 2007).

23 Ashley Graves Lanfer & Madeleine Taylor, *Immigrant Engagement in Public Open Space: Strategies for the New Boston* (Barr Foundation, 2010).

24 Dines, et al., *Public Spaces and Social Relations in East London*.

25 Bloomfield & Bianchini, *Planning for the Cosmopolitan City*, 6.

26 Sandeep Kumar & George Martin, "A Case for Culturally Responsive Urban Design," *Ontario Planning Journal* 19, no. 5 (2004).

27 Julie Guthman, "If They Only Knew: Color Blindness and Universalism in California Alternative Food Institutions," *The Professional Geographer* 60, no. 3 (2008): 388.

28 Lownsbrough & Beunderman, *Equally Spaced?*

29 Ali Madanipour, *Whose Public Space?* (Routledge, 2010), 11.

30 Zoe Sofoulis, et al., *Out & About in Penrith: Universal Design and Cultural Context* (University of Western Sydney & Penrith City Council, 2008).

31 Clare Rishbeth, Farnaz Ganji & Goran Vodicka, "Ethnographic Understandings of Ethnically Diverse Neighbourhoods to Inform Urban Design Practice," *Local Environment: The International Journal of Justice and Sustainability* 23, no. 1 (2018): 14.

32 Yasminah Beebeejaun, "The Participation Trap: The Limitations of Participation for Ethnic and Racial Groups," *International Planning Studies* 11, no. 1 (2006): 79.

33 Lownsbrough & Beunderman, *Equally Spaced?*

34 Fred Kent, *Placemaking Around the World* (Urban Land, 2008).

35 CABE Space, *Helping Community Groups to Improve Public Spaces* (Commission for Architecture and the Built Environment, 2007).

36 Kumar & Martin, "A Case for Culturally Responsive Urban Design."

37 Blake van Velden & Dory Reeves, "Intercultural Public Spaces," paper presented at the International Planning Conference, Christchurch, New Zealand (April 20, 2010).

38 CABE Space, *Community Green: Using local spaces to tackle inequality and improve health* (Commission for Architecture and the Built Environment, 2010).

39 Low et al., *Rethinking Urban Parks*; Sofoulis et al., *Out & About in Penrith*.

40 Lownsbrough & Beunderman, *Equally Spaced?*

backgrounds. Designers can create spaces that resemble "home," such as the Ryerson University student-led designs based on Bollywood for the Gerrard India Bazaar, an ethnic business enclave in East Toronto.[36] Officials can also assign culturally relevant names (toponyms) in order to promote a specific sense of identity;[37] two examples of this practice include the renaming of Mount McKinley (Alaska) as Denali, and Ayers Rock (Australia), as Uluru. Inclusive spaces must provide appropriate seating (not the "standard" park bench) for individuals or the nuclear family, and also for extended families and groups of individuals simply hoping to socialize. Safety is a major barrier to park usage: people report feeling unsafe in spaces with overgrown vegetation, insufficient lighting, and high walls.[38]

Design and utility blend easily.[39] Sometimes simply better design and/or maintenance of existing facilities can resolve problems, instead of building new facilities.[40] Therefore, the "use" stage of open space development must include proper maintenance and management of facilities. Additionally, open-space staff must adopt new, culturally competent approaches to interacting with diverse users. Hiring staff who resemble users or who speak the language of users can go far in reducing perceptions of discrimination, which has been shown to be an important deterrent. Targeted marketing strategies could also be used to respond to the diverse needs of various groups in order to re-establish a park as a welcoming place for all.[41]

Accessibility depends not only on the location of parks, but also on the built environment that surrounds them. Good street lighting, adequate sidewalks, street interconnectivity, local land use, infrastructure, and facility maintenance all influence when and how urban residents participate in outdoor recreation.[42] Numerous studies, especially in the United States and United Kingdom, have demonstrated spatial injustice: that there are fewer accessible parks and public spaces in economically disadvantaged areas. In addition, the parks and spaces in these neighborhoods also tend to be of lower quality, making quantity and quality especially important in low-income communities.[43] If the community is not helping "set the table" during the design process, spaces attempting to cater to everyone can tend to be impersonal.

Toward Culturally Inclusive Practice

What is the role of the planning and urban design professional in the shift toward interculturalism? It is important to note that the professions most closely associated with the policy, planning, design, and development of public and open spaces are not known for their difference, diversity, or cultural heterogeneity. Rishbeth et al. are unequivocal, hypothesizing that, "findings from ethnographic research can provide a resource that improves cultural literacy and supports social justice in professional practice."[44]

I concur. There is a solid case to be made that the training and recruitment of professionals who more fully reflect the make-up of our, "cities of difference," would help speed the production, quality, and maintenance of culturally inclusive spaces, and, critically, the embedding and mainstreaming of culturally inclusive practice within those professions.[45] Until that mainstreaming happens, current professionals must take added care to ensure that they embark on culturally inclusive practice where difference and diversity are intentional and are represented throughout the design process.

The move toward physical distancing, however long it lasts, will require rethinking our policies and plans for public spaces, but it must not diminish our resolve to develop more culturally inclusive spaces. Elsewhere, I have taken a necessarily broad look at what these plans might look like through the lenses of space as security, resistance, and possibility.[46] I argued that the sense of possibility and hope that was emerging in democratic and democratizing projects, spaces, and places around the world could serve as models to inform the creation of new spaces of mixing, engagement, and encounter to lessen social distancing, isolation, and segregation. Here, I am adding another layer by arguing that the provision of high-quality culturally inclusive spaces is essential in any society that "embodies a dynamic and multi-faceted culture."[47]

However, we must not fall into a deterministic trap: we must recognize the limits of design to solve deep social injustices. There are two aspects to this. First, as Phil Wood and Charles Landry point out:

> The intercultural city depends on more than a *design challenge*. It derives from a central notion that people are developing a shared future whereby each individual feels they have something to contribute in shaping, making and co-creating a joint endeavor. A thousand tiny transformations will create an atmosphere in public space that feels open and where all feel safe and valued.[48]

Second, as Jason Byrne and Jennifer Wolch note: "The cultural landscape perspective shows us how landscapes can become racialized, shifting the scale of environmental injustice from the home, the factory, or the neighborhood to entire landscapes."[49]

In addition, community-based planning processes surrounding open space may foster collaboration during planning sessions but may not radically alter the lack of power of disadvantaged participants after the process has concluded.[50] Similarly, there is a threat that residents engaged in planning for open space may create more exclusive, rather than more inclusive, spaces.[51] Clearly, there is a role for the planner to advocate on behalf of inclusivity and coproduction, recognizing that this may require different treatment of individuals and groups based on need.

Let's start from a position of humility. Do we want to live in a world where we tolerate the tedium and misery of cities of *in*difference, with limited mixing, engagement, and encounter, or do we want to live in cities where we recognize, understand, and engage with difference, diversity, and cultural heterogeneity that could transform civic institutions, the public realm, its discourses, and city management practices? As Wood and Landry argue: "If we want the intercultural city, we cannot leave it to chance."[52]

Author Postscript: This paper was written prior to the racist murder of George Floyd, by police, at the intersection of Chicago Avenue and East 38th Street in Minneapolis on May 25, 2020.

41 Arnold & Shinew, "The Role of Gender, Race, and Income on Park Use Constraints."

42 Talen, *Design for Diversity*; Juan Sanchez, "An Assessment and Analysis of Issues and Patterns Associated with the Utilization of Open Spaces by Latino Immigrants in an Urban Neighborhood in Boston," Master's Thesis, Department of Urban and Environmental Policy and Planning, Tufts University (2010).

43 CABE, *Urban Green Nation: Building the evidence base* (Commission for Architecture and the Built Environment, 2010).

44 Rishbeth, et al., "Ethnographic Understandings," 1.

45 Fincher & Jacobs, *Cities of Difference*.

46 Julian Agyeman, *Introducing Just Sustainabilities: Policy, Planning, and Practice* (Zed Books Ltd, 2013).

47 Clare Rishbeth, "Ethnic Minority Groups and the Design of Public Open Space: An Inclusive Landscape?" *Landscape Research* 26, no. 4 (2001): 364.

48 Phil Wood & Charles Landry, *The Intercultural City: Planning for Diversity Advantage* (Earthscan, 2012), 260 (my emphasis).

49 Jason Byrne & Jennifer Wolch, "Nature, Race, and Parks: Past Research and Future Directions for Geographic Research," *Progress in Human Geography* 33, no. 6 (2009): 743, 756.

50 Beebejaun, "The Participation Trap."

51 Ibid.

52 Wood & Landry, *The Intercultural City*, 320.

Acknowledgment: Thanks to my student Laurent Xavier Frapaise for his meticulous editing and formatting of this paper.

DESIGN JUSTICE Q+A

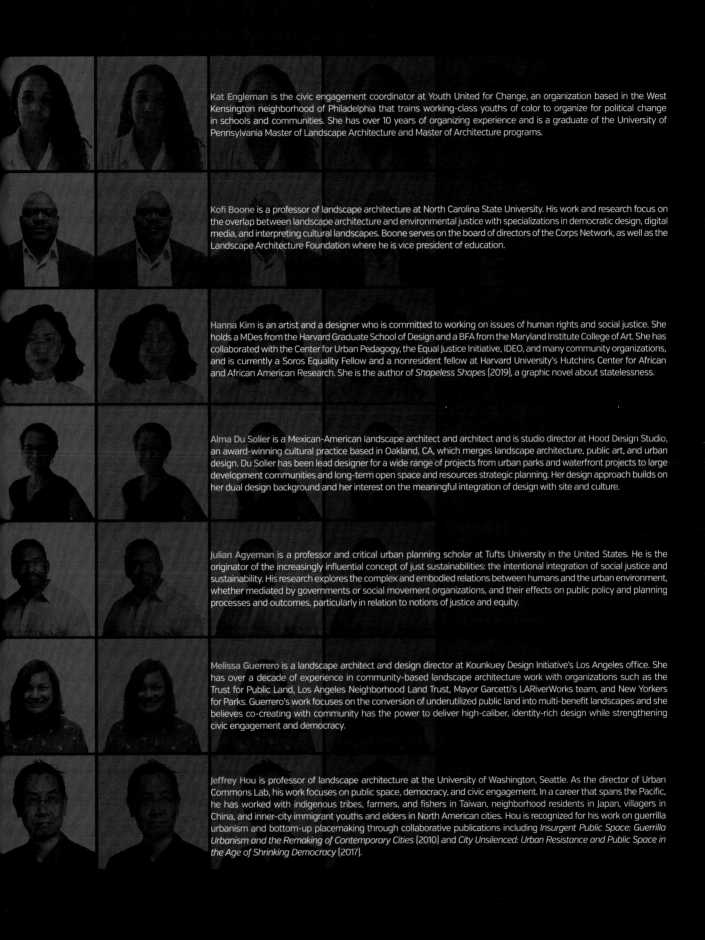

Kat Engleman is the civic engagement coordinator at Youth United for Change, an organization based in the West Kensington neighborhood of Philadelphia that trains working-class youths of color to organize for political change in schools and communities. She has over 10 years of organizing experience and is a graduate of the University of Pennsylvania Master of Landscape Architecture and Master of Architecture programs.

Kofi Boone is a professor of landscape architecture at North Carolina State University. His work and research focus on the overlap between landscape architecture and environmental justice with specializations in democratic design, digital media, and interpreting cultural landscapes. Boone serves on the board of directors of the Corps Network, as well as the Landscape Architecture Foundation where he is vice president of education.

Hanna Kim is an artist and a designer who is committed to working on issues of human rights and social justice. She holds a MDes from the Harvard Graduate School of Design and a BFA from the Maryland Institute College of Art. She has collaborated with the Center for Urban Pedagogy, the Equal Justice Initiative, IDEO, and many community organizations, and is currently a Soros Equality Fellow and a nonresident fellow at Harvard University's Hutchins Center for African and African American Research. She is the author of *Shapeless Shapes* (2019), a graphic novel about statelessness.

Alma Du Solier is a Mexican-American landscape architect and architect and is studio director at Hood Design Studio, an award-winning cultural practice based in Oakland, CA, which merges landscape architecture, public art, and urban design. Du Solier has been lead designer for a wide range of projects from urban parks and waterfront projects to large development communities and long-term open space and resources strategic planning. Her design approach builds on her dual design background and her interest on the meaningful integration of design with site and culture.

Julian Agyeman is a professor and critical urban planning scholar at Tufts University in the United States. He is the originator of the increasingly influential concept of just sustainabilities: the intentional integration of social justice and sustainability. His research explores the complex and embodied relations between humans and the urban environment, whether mediated by governments or social movement organizations, and their effects on public policy and planning processes and outcomes, particularly in relation to notions of justice and equity.

Melissa Guerrero is a landscape architect and design director at Kounkuey Design Initiative's Los Angeles office. She has over a decade of experience in community-based landscape architecture work with organizations such as the Trust for Public Land, Los Angeles Neighborhood Land Trust, Mayor Garcetti's LARiverWorks team, and New Yorkers for Parks. Guerrero's work focuses on the conversion of underutilized public land into multi-benefit landscapes and she believes co-creating with community has the power to deliver high-caliber, identity-rich design while strengthening civic engagement and democracy.

Jeffrey Hou is professor of landscape architecture at the University of Washington, Seattle. As the director of Urban Commons Lab, his work focuses on public space, democracy, and civic engagement. In a career that spans the Pacific, he has worked with indigenous tribes, farmers, and fishers in Taiwan, neighborhood residents in Japan, villagers in China, and inner-city immigrant youths and elders in North American cities. Hou is recognized for his work on guerrilla urbanism and bottom-up placemaking through collaborative publications including *Insurgent Public Space: Guerrilla Urbanism and the Remaking of Contemporary Cities* (2010) and *City Unsilenced: Urban Resistance and Public Space in the Age of Shrinking Democracy* (2017).

We are in a moment of reckoning. The global pandemic has drawn the curtain back on the racial and socioeconomic inequities that have always been in place, disproportionately ravaging already vulnerable BIPOC populations. Since the birth of the Occupy Movement in 2011 and Black Lives Matter in 2013, civil unrest over these growing inequities has continued to simmer through the decade. COVID-19's swift public health crisis, economic shutdown, and subsequent loss of jobs served to bring the pre-existing simmer to a boil. Under these conditions, George Floyd's brutal murder at the hands of police officer Derek Chauvin became a catalyst for national and international uprising.

In direct contrast to the sudden emptying of public space that characterized the beginning of the pandemic, since those eight minutes and 46 seconds on May 25, 2020 we've seen city streets occupied by protestors in solidarity, the overnight creation of informal spaces for healing and remembrance, the establishment of autonomous zones, the reclamation of spaces that memorialized racists, and the increased need for accessible green spaces in every neighborhood. Uses and expressions of space and power are being redefined, and design students, academics, and professionals alike are calling for design justice, new methods of learning from and meaningfully engaging with communities, and full accountability within our practices that have long histories of spatial injustice against and oppression of Black and Brown people. The call is not new, but the moment demands new types of design processes and outputs that will contribute to an inclusive and equitable future. Allison Nkwocha asked seven design justice advocates to consider what these new types of design processes might be and where they might lead.

Design fields have a history of treating ommunity engagement as a box to eck rather than an essential source of eativity, learning, and empowerment. ow can designers shift from designing r to designing *with*?

Kat Engleman: Society develops all of us to see ourselves as either the people who make decisions or the people who have no agency in what happens to them and the world around them. Designers often play into this dynamic as people who typically already have class and race privilege and utilize their role to show that *they* are the experts and *they* are the ones who make the decisions. Additionally, when it comes time to engage communities, we ask groups of people to gather and share their individual opinions about the project as opposed to engaging them in a collective decision-making process. We can't design *with* communities if our process prioritizes designers and then individual members over the community as a unit. I think in order to change this dynamic, designers have to create processes that allow community members to regularly participate in the decision-making processes themselves, to do so as a collective, and to have their decisions respected as the project moves forward. This transforms the designer's role from being transactional and hierarchical to one that is mutual, allowing designers to use their expertise as a conduit while community members step into ownership of the projects that will impact their lives.

Kofi Boone: I think some of this is about trust. Establishing trust takes time and accountability. Engagement doesn't mean empowerment or even satisfaction. The scope of a lot of professional work compresses trust-building into the timeframe of a project. I think in some cases there is a need for sustained trust-building with communities, uncoupled from the timeframe of a project, especially if they have been harmed in the past by well-intended design and planning work. And I think some of this is about power. Much of the research that forms the basis of community work is decades old when government policy was stronger and more resources were local or at least regional. Now, fewer resources used for change in the landscape are local, policies have weakened, trust has diminished. Meeting the needs of local people when resources are not local, on land that local people do not own, is very difficult. There are some useful strategies coming from partnerships that empower communities with local land and policy control.

Hanna Kim: I believe that at the core of any design practice lies an ability to create genuine and lasting relationships. Too often, however, the role of a designer becomes distorted in a capitalist, white supremacist, and patriarchal society. When designers aren't taught to or allowed to access the power and responsibility inherent in design, they can easily be relegated to a middleperson between a client and a community. To combat this, designers must realize the true potential and ramifications that exist at their fingertips. Designers don't just create buildings – buildings create cities, and cities create nations. Designers don't just create posters – posters create messages, and messages create ideologies. For me, this is both empowering and humbling. It is also scary. "Designing with" needs honest and rigorous interrogation. Who is included in the design process? How will this design impact generations of communities? Where are the blind spots? What are the unintended consequences? Who are the real experts here? Participatory design offers great guidance on this topic. Ultimately, I believe it comes down to having humility to listen and unlearn, exercising moral courage to be on the right side of history, and taking time to build genuine trust and solidarity with people.

Alma Du Solier: I do not believe designers today intentionally follow a community process to check a box. Most believe the process we are following is inclusive and helpful, and, if asked, most would say we would do it even if not required. But changing the default of "designing for" to "designing with" requires us also to question our process constantly and tailor it to the idiosyncrasies of particular communities. Identifying a community's unique stories requires research by inquisitive and brave designers and clients. Research allows us to meet the community at a place of respect and appreciation for what works and what does not seem to work. But, our understanding of place based on research is only part of it – we still need to be prepared to change it based on the community's input. This suggests that the engagement process should not only be part of a project's initial stage. We let ourselves believe we cannot collect relevant input at all project stages because we confuse engagement with seeking design direction, and thus stop engagement when the design has been "frozen" to avoid changes that could contradict approved permits or budgets. "Designing with" requires us to focus on community values and continue dialogue to evaluate our interpretation of such values in our work throughout.

Julian Agyeman: I'd like to see much more use of urban ethnographies by designers and planners. In my Department of Urban and Environmental Policy and Planning at Tufts, we have a very popular class on Urban Ethnography for Urban Planners. Every school of design, planning, architecture, etc., should have such a class. Deep ethnographic data should be coproduced by designers and communities before projects start. I see this as the only way to forge greater community understandings that can help designers and planners shift from designing *for* to designing *with*. Designing *with* is coproduced design.

Melissa Guerrero: For far too long, too many communities have been left out of the design process altogether, and the history of urban planning is rife with examples of so-called "master plans" concocted in offices without any community input. More recently, design and planning have included local community voices, but, as you indicate, this can be too proscribed. At Kounkuey Design Initiative (KDI), we have set out to create a new way of involving the community as an integral part of the design process, from start to finish. For each project the community engagement process is tailor-made for that community and site, but the common denominator for each is to start with the premise that the community has an expertise just as valuable as a sub-consultant's or the client's. This simple switch in how we value the community's expertise leads to engagement strategies that respect their contributions such as paying for their time, developing a leadership council to advise on the engagement work plan, and developing a committed group of residents who meet regularly to discuss larger neighborhood issues related to the public space project we're asking them to co-create with us.

Jeffrey Hou: Indeed, community engagement has often become procedural and lacking in substance even with the best intention. In *Design as Democracy* (Island Press, 2017), a group of colleagues and I assembled a collection of techniques that focus on community engagement as a source of creativity, learning, and empowerment. But beyond just techniques, we need to change the way we work with communities – to learn from the perspectives of those who have more extensive knowledge and experience. Besides taking on projects from public or private clients, we need to proactively develop projects and initiatives in partnership with community organizations. Shifting from designing *for* to designing *with* requires a fundamental shift in mindset and an awareness of our limits as design professionals. We need to consider public engagement as an essential part of the design process – a dialogical process that enables the stakeholders (designers included) to communicate and deliberate what the issues and solutions are. We need to build relationships with community stakeholders and see them as partners in the process. It is not feasible for design professionals to develop a full understanding of issues and nuances in a short amount of time. It is therefore essential that we work *with* our community partners.

+ What does authentically inclusive community space look like? Can you cite any exemplary projects in terms of the process of community engagement and how it manifested in the outcome?

Kat Engleman: I think these types of spaces are ones that are have a level of specificity that grounds it in a time, place, and people. An authentic and inclusive community space where I live will have to be different than a space that is across the city, not just because the physical locations are different but because the people and built environment bring experiences and histories that produce something fundamentally different here than they would anywhere else. The depth of this specificity doesn't have to automatically be understandable to "outsiders," but it should be legible to the people who would use those spaces. I also think these types of spaces are ones that allow people to be in their full dignity. Can it be an inclusive space if community members inherently feel ashamed of their class position? Or if someone with a disability cannot fully use a space? Or if a person of color is hypervigilant about the racial dynamics in the space? Unfortunately, I haven't seen many spaces like this, and typically spaces like this are ones that are created by community members themselves without designers.

Kofi Boone: I don't know. Years ago I would've said it's a space that attracts a wide array of people who feel they can be their authentic selves in public and can negotiate differences in non-violent ways. The cliché is something like Washington Square Park in New York City, where you can hear many languages, see a hip-hop cipher, a protest, a Chinese holiday celebration, etc. Today, I'd say that spaces don't operate in vacuums and I question the possibility of inclusive spaces in decidedly exclusive communities. Recently I've been learning more about the origins of the Black Commons and Community Land Trusts. Fannie Lou Hamer's Freedom Farm Cooperative had characteristics of authentically inclusive space. Co-op members had stakes on the shared space and its products. Cooperative economics, governance, and power. I think these spaces may be more recognizable by their contexts and underlying processes than their forms and artifacts. I remember an email exchange with Susan Fainstein about the components of her Just City theory. Her theory references the significance of systems: affordable housing, equitable transportation, and a living wage. Why not landscapes? She said she'd never thought of them in that way. Toni Griffin has been pursuing this question for a long time and is creating interesting and not-so-obvious connections between people and their environments. Mindy Thompson Fullilove as well. I can't think of a space per se or its physical characteristics; but I try to think about inclusive spaces as being surrounded by communities engaged in inclusive practices.

Hanna Kim: Every community has its own structures, dynamics, and strategies. However, the communities that center those who experience firsthand or who are directly impacted seem to cultivate the most inclusive and sustainable relationships and the most creative outcomes. I've been working with two organizations recently on projects that seek to engage and represent community. The first is the Convict Leasing and Labor Project (founded by activist and historian Reginald Moore), which seeks to expose the history and legacy of the convict leasing system. With Mr. Moore's guidance, I produced a report on the "Sugar Land 95" – the remains of 95 African Americans unearthed in Sugar Land, Texas in 2018. In this case, the directly impacted community–the victims of convict leasing–are no longer able to speak their stories. For years, CLLP has been holding people accountable so that the descendants of the Sugar Land 95 could be identified. History, memory, and trauma can expand the notion of inclusivity in the community design process. Another organization I've been working with is United Stateless – a grassroots organization led by stateless activists in the US. Stateless people are often forced to live in the shadows because of lack of identification and as a result they may be ignored in community engagement processes for public projects. These people face a dilemma: speaking up proves their existence, but it also makes them more vulnerable to state violence; using aliases protects their identity but perpetuates their feeling of erasure. I've been working on ways to overcome this through illustration – sometimes just being seen can be a form of justice.

Alma Du Solier: The inclusive process is one that engages a community in dialogue about values and true aspirations, not paving colors, furniture styles, or endless wish-lists of arbitrary programs. The latter approach reduces the process to a Pinterest search for pretty pictures instead of what really matters. It may appear inclusive because everybody is invited to provide opinions, but they are superficial. I had the opportunity to be lead consultant in developing a master plan for Ocean Beach, the Pacific coast of San Francisco. Thirty-five stakeholder groups with diverse backgrounds and agendas were represented on a task force. There was a key topic dividing the group: the relocation of a sewage pipe that was perceived as the cause of and solution to the problem, depending on who you asked. We created a process to understand the values behind this divided view and were able to elevate the conversation to serving those values, instead of finding a compromise on the solution. Three different implementation plans have emerged from this process, building on the value-serving "key moves" proposed by the master plan. For a site with this level of physical and jurisdictional complexity, the change toward realizing aspirations per agreed-upon values instead of fighting over engineering approaches provided a productive and truly inclusive process that has yielded win-win solutions.

Julian Agyeman: One of the classic cases of urban place-making from a low-income, minority perspective is the redevelopment of Dudley Street by the Dudley Street Neighborhood Initiative (DSNI). Dudley Street straddles the Roxbury–Dorchester line in Boston and DSNI's 34-member board of directors is diverse, with equal representation of the community's four major cultures (and therefore historical narratives of place): African American, Cape Verdean, Latinx, and white. It works to implement resident-driven plans with partners including community development corporations, other non-profit organizations, and religious institutions serving the neighborhood, banks, government agencies, businesses, and foundations. DSNI soon realized that retaining community-driven development would not be sufficient to halt the kind of gentrification that now displaces residents in other parts of Boston. Its solution was the creation of a community land trust, Dudley Neighbors, Inc. (DNI), which uses a 99-year ground lease that restricts resale prices in order to keep the land available for affordable housing. To date, a total of 200 new homes and two community spaces or micro-centers have been built on DNI land.

Melissa Guerrero: At Kounkuey Design Initiative (KDI) we hold the goal of creating equitable and sustainable development with communities in every single project, but we also realize that design alone cannot solve inequity. This is why we developed the "Productive Public Space" model that integrates community organizing, cultural and income-generating programs, research, design, and planning to holistically help disadvantaged communities build healthier, more connected, and more prosperous neighborhoods and cities. All of our projects are case studies for how to conduct authentic community engagement that guides the designed outcome, but I'll focus on one park project, Nuestro Lugar (Our Place) in North Shore, California as an example. Staff from KDI's design, planning, and community teams worked together on delivering dozens of community engagements. One key workshop was co-led with artists where the conversation was focused on what residents loved about their community. The park's theme "From Sea to Sky" emerged and it's reflected in the landforms for stargazing, the plant palette, wayfinding signs, a community mural, and symbols embedded throughout the park. With KDI's support residents also established a women-led food cooperative, a youth-led bike share program, and an arts committee. The park includes an allée that doubles as a flexible market space to support these collectives and more to come. Completed in 2018, the park marks the beginning of a new era for North Shore: one in which community members can gather, play, celebrate their heritage, and call for more of the improvements they need.

Jeffrey Hou: To me, an authentically inclusive community space is community owned and reflective of the social, cultural, and economic diversity of the community. It is also evolving and open-ended. Furthermore, it must be a place of learning and understanding. By community owned I mean a sense of ownership the comes from engagement in the process of placemaking. Because a community can change and its boundaries can shift, an authentically inclusive community must have the capacity to evolve. As inclusivity takes time and effort to develop, an inclusive community space needs to serve as a place of learning and understanding. Growing Hing Hay Park is a project in Seattle's Chinatown International District that I have co-chaired since 2013. Through the design process, we faced conflicting interests from diverse community stakeholders. We had the fortune of working with Turenscape and MIG to develop a design that gave form to the complexity of cultural identities in the neighborhood. But community engagement as a learning process goes beyond just the design. After the project was completed, representatives from different community groups continued to develop a signage design that eventually embraced the multicultural identities in the neighborhood. Both the process and design made the park an authentically inclusive community space.

+ This is not the first time that mainstream design culture has been "awakened" to the importance of recognizing BIPOC communities and the landscapes that shape them. Do you see this as an enduring shift in design?

Kat Engleman: The pessimist in me says no. A more optimistic view would be that it's too soon to tell. There's an ever-heightening level of political polarization in the US, which has moved some people into understanding the ways racial capitalism has produced various types of conditions for people of color with many others pushing back on the idea that racism is alive. It'd be naïve to think that the design profession doesn't also hold this spectrum within it that will inevitably hold back progressive movement. Additionally, power structures are extremely adept at absorbing these types of pushes in order to maintain the fundamental structure while pacifying people by offering limited and symbolic gestures toward change. An example of this is the painting of "black lives matter" on city streets while not actually structurally changing the conditions that produce police brutality. In the case of design, I fear that the momentum we see will simply become about merely "recognizing" race and racism or representational politics as opposed to a deep understanding of how we all understand our role within the current power structures and seek to radically transform it.

Kofi Boone: I think there is a lot of interest and increasing awareness. I think there is a sense that the story we've told ourselves about the value of landscapes and communities is incomplete. Whether or not this translates into resources to protect, nurture, and grow BIPOC communities remains to be seen. Despite the current situation with COVID, our global momentum is spinning toward increased segregation, disparities, and risks based on race. These challenges remain. What I am seeing is an increase in the level of agency young BIPOC designers are exercising in the face of this wave of attention. I think that the past few years have been a golden age for almost all of the art and design fields for BIPOC people except architecture and landscape architecture. There is something pernicious about the barriers within those fields that don't seem to extend as strongly to other fields. I see young people seeking out different relationships and practice models with BIPOC communities than mainstream practice models that come with the baggage of bias and constraint. I think the question for the rest of us is what is our role in supporting them as they redefine who could and should be in front working with BIPOC communities and not just how we do so.

Hanna Kim: Since George Floyd's murder, I see toolkits, workshops, and manifestos popping up all over social media. Corporations and organizations have put out statements on how they are standing with the BIPOC community [some get it right and some don't]. The removal of monuments has been truly inspiring. While I celebrate these changes, I always try to remember the strong grip of hegemony and history. The people may be "awakened," but the machine is still at work benefitting the already-rich and polarizing the public. That's why we must stay vigilant, malleable, and hopeful. Centering BIPOC voices and creating reparative opportunities for historically marginalized communities are critical steps. More importantly, a thorough assessment of our privilege and radical reimagination of our role should be a constant effort rather than a one-time response. Mierle Laderman Ukeles's "Maintenance Art" manifesto helped me reimagine my practice as one of maintenance, rather than development. Activists who get in "good trouble" (thank you, Rep. John Lewis) despite disappointment and suffering, exemplify what an "enduring shift" truly looks like. We can let their wisdom guide us through the unprecedented times. It may be difficult to know where we are right now, but we should all strive to stay awake.

Alma Du Solier: I certainly hope it's enduring. I believe the strongest challenge to recognizing the values of our BIPOC communities is our fear of controversy. We have not developed tools to discuss difficult topics that sometimes are key to revealing the true essence of place. We set our processes to achieve consensus at all cost, simplifying questions to the lowest common denominator where easily achieved agreement is possible and taking input from whomever shows up to the meetings, even if there isn't full representation. We need all at the table and what draws the most active participation sometimes is controversy. I am not advocating for creating controversy, but rather for honestly questioning our "cookie-cutter" processes and for not being afraid to ask difficult questions and present difficult topics, such as the legacy of past government actions that have physically divided a place and still hinder investment funding, or the best value of open space in the face of widespread homelessness, to name just two. We need to get creative finding ways to discuss these topics openly, moving away from false dichotomies pinned as mutually exclusive. Dialogue leads to better understanding of issues and each other. Our role as facilitators of inclusion is one of brave co-creators, not surveyors of shallow and "safe" visual preferences.

Julian Agyeman: BIPOC communities are not only shaped by landscapes, they shape them too! From an urban planning perspective, I see this particular iteration of getting "woke" as deeper and more fundamental than earlier ones for three reasons. First, the Black Lives Matter movement has permeated our collective consciousness more deeply and across all racial/ethnic groups, especially whites, than before. Second, and related, this is the social media age. Nothing gets a pass. Everything is recorded in some way. Third, the urban planning/design narrative is changing. We are not mincing words anymore. In a recent piece in *The Conversation*, I called out urban planning as the spatial toolkit of white supremacy. Racial segregation was not the byproduct of urban planning; it was, in many cases, its intention – it was not by accident, but by design. This may have been contested 20 to 30 years ago, but is less so today.

Melissa Guerrero: As designers and planners working on behalf of BIPOC communities, we must actively work to make it an enduring change. When necessary, we need to be ready and willing to educate clients and funders, whether that be on a project-by-project basis or on a larger scale through policy advocacy work. Changing education will be fundamental, both in terms of curriculum and student body. The more we can make design schools inclusive and diverse, the more the design and planning professions will better reflect the communities they serve, making this an enduring pivot rather than a flash-in-the-pan concern.

Jeffrey Hou: The moment of "awakening" in 2020 is unlike others in recent memories in terms of its depth and scope. Whether the shift or interest will endure or not will depend on every one of us – faculty, academic administrators, students, practitioners, activists, organizers, and so on. Efforts need to come from both top and bottom. We need to put pressure on the professional organizations, universities, and institutions to take appropriate actions, to reallocate resources, and to address longstanding biases and disparities in education and practice. As educators and practitioners, every one of us needs to be accountable. But efforts also need to come from those who may not in the position of power and authority. The moment will only become an enduring movement if enough people are engaged and take action. The power of the movement comes from our individual and collective engagement. It can start with a group project in the studio, a volunteer effort outside the classroom, and/or participation in a local or national event, such as Design as Protest. A transformative and enduring change depends on all of us.

IN CONVERSATION WITH

PAUL PATON

+

ANNE-MARIE PISANI

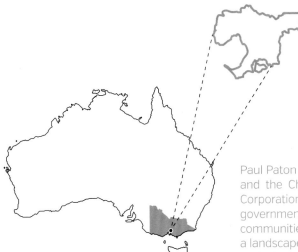

Paul Paton is a Gunnai, Monaro, and Gunditjmara man from South-Eastern Australia and the Chief Executive Officer at the Federation of Victorian Traditional Owner Corporations. He has had a long-standing career in not-for-profit organizations and government working together with Traditional Custodians to help facilitate Indigenous communities' self-determination and connection to their lands. Anne-Marie Pisani is a landscape architect with experience in projects at multiple scales across the public and private sectors. She has been recognized by the Australian Institute of Landscape Architects for her contribution to the field by developing processes for engagement with Aboriginal and Torres Strait Islander communities. Also partners in life, Paul and Anne-Marie are strong advocates for the inclusion of Aboriginal ways of knowing, being, and doing within the planning and design of urban and natural environments. Sara Padgett Kjaersgaard interviewed them for the LA+ COMMUNITY issue.

+ Aboriginal and Torres Strait Australia is diverse, both in language and landscape. Can you explain and situate this for people not familiar with Australia?

PP The Australian landscape holds the imprint of thousands of generations of Aboriginal people. Aboriginal people occupied the Australian continent for tens of thousands of years prior to European settlement living a lifestyle rich in culture, developed through a varied and complex set of languages, tribal alliances, trading routes, beliefs, and social customs that involved totemism, superstition, initiation, burial rites, and tribal moieties that regulated relationships and marriage.

These cultural practices involve a deep spiritual understanding of the environment and govern how Aboriginal communities live with and maintain the land, plants, and animals of their region. Stories are linked with culture as a way of passing information to younger generations. The stories often talk about creation and explain how natural elements were formed or how species came to be. Included in these stories can be knowledge of hunting locations, animal behaviors, and any restrictions or laws that apply to a species or region. Understanding the land through seasonal observations was once essential to survival and is today, essential to management. The arrival of Europeans irrevocably changed the lives of Aboriginal groups – effects that are still being felt today.

+ The recent Yarra River Protection (Wilip-gin Birrarung murron) Act 2017 recognizes the intrinsic connection of the Wurundjeri peoples to Melbourne's Yarra River and its Country. How does this legislation highlight Indigenous understanding of land and what is its significance in broader discussions about sustainability?

PP First, I should mention that for Australian Aboriginal people the term "Country" incorporates the physical, cultural, and spiritual landscape as one. It includes what's under the ground, on the ground, above the ground, in the sky, and the cosmos. The Birrarung (Yarra River) is connected to Wurundjeri culture spiritually through their creation stories, particularly the river as a life source that was etched into the landscape by their ancestral creator spirit Bunjil, the wedge-tailed eagle. The Birrarung–which in Wurundjeri language means "shadows of the mists"–flows approximately 240 km from the Yarra Valley into Port Phillip Bay passing through many wetlands, which were great sources of food and water, where Melbourne and its immediate suburbs now stand. Wurundjeri people once moved freely around the area based on the seasons and the availability of food. In winter, the Wurundjeri-willam clan regularly camped in the higher areas as the land near the river flooded. In spring and summer, they travelled more frequently, hunting and gathering food and visiting sacred sites.

Their spiritual connection to the many special places in the area extends back thousands of years through periods of extraordinary environmental upheaval that saw dramatic changes in the river. These stories of environmental change have been passed on through generations that enabled a highly attuned understanding of how to live sustainably and ensure that the land remains healthy. The Yarra River Protection (Wilip-gin Birrarung murron) Act is a positive step forward in recognizing the river as an entity unto itself and water as the provider of life to the land and its people. It also ensures that the rich knowledge that has been accumulated and passed on over those thousands of generations isn't lost and is able to inform how we manage waterways now and into the future.

+ Australia has a number of different legal processes enabling Aboriginal people to claim traditional ownership of their ancestral lands and to protect their cultural heritage. Is there a difference between the work you do with communities who have a formal determination of traditional ownership in comparison to those that haven't?

AP I believe it is important to be as inclusive as possible when working with Aboriginal communities. In the [southern Australian] state of Victoria, there are currently 11 Traditional Owner groups (or "Registered Aboriginal Parties") recognized by the Aboriginal Heritage Act, which have responsibility for managing and protecting Aboriginal cultural heritage in their ancestral Country. There are also a number of Aboriginal Corporations across the state that undertake a vital representative role for their communities, but which are not formally recognized under the Aboriginal Heritage Act.

Clients sometimes provide direction to only engage with the parties recognized under the Aboriginal Heritage Act. This can be a difficult situation: although Registered Aboriginal Parties have gone to great lengths to confirm their ongoing connections to their Country through court proceedings, this doesn't mean that other Aboriginal groups have any less connection to Country. Being inclusive through engaging with all of these groups shows the community that we understand that the official recognition of groups is a colonial construct and that we recognize and acknowledge the deep connection that all Aboriginal people have with Country.

PP Traditional Owners have inherent cultural rights to maintain their cultural practices alongside specific cultural obligations to care for Country. It is the obligation of the states under the United Nations Declaration of Rights of Indigenous Peoples (UNDRIP) to support these. Formal recognition gives states confidence that they are dealing with the appropriate people who hold those connections, but it can also leave gaps in consultation processes where groups haven't achieved this status. States need to increase their capabilities in order to engage with all communities. From an Aboriginal community perspective, our personal relationships and connections have stood the test of time through thousands of generations to the point of us knowing who is connected to where and how. It is, however, important that consultation isn't confused with recognition and there would be possible implications if the two aren't clearly defined throughout the process. The bottom line is that there must be equity and opportunity provided to all irrespective of status, and the only way to achieve this is through increasing one's own capability to know who the communities are and establishing relationships with them.

+ The state of Victoria has a high number of joint management plans with Traditional Owners. What are the cultural and ecological benefits of this type of land management?

PP Joint management is a formal partnership arrangement between Traditional Owners and the state where both share their knowledge to manage specific national parks and other protected areas. Government agencies with land management responsibilities for Victoria's state and national parks work together with Registered Aboriginal Parties to enable the knowledge and culture of the Traditional Owners to be recognized through participation in the decision-making and management of public land.

The cultural benefits of these arrangements are such that, similar to the Yarra Protection Act, traditional knowledge which has been accumulated and passed on through generations is able to be incorporated into the ongoing management of land. This, in turn, recognizes and restores the stewardship that Aboriginal people hold toward "caring for Country" – a traditional role that is integral to both community and individual health.

The Australian landscape is unique, with ecosystems that have been influenced and sustainably managed by Aboriginal people for tens of thousands of years. The arrival of Europeans has had a dramatic effect on the landscape, largely due to introduced land management practices that weren't appropriate to this place. Large-scale clearing of land for farming, European agricultural practices, and water diversion from the landscape are just a few examples of significant change that have had detrimental effects on the land. Another is the failure to recognize the importance of traditional practices of controlled burning used by Aboriginal people to reduce the risk of unmanageable bushfires and to regenerate flora. Joint management is a mechanism to reintroduce traditional knowledge and practice and hopefully reverse some of these effects. The enormous destruction of the 2019 bushfires throughout Australia is a clear example of this impact on the landscape to both flora and fauna.

+ Can you tell us about any specific methodologies you employ that enable you to undertake work with Aboriginal communities more successfully?

AP When I am engaging with Aboriginal communities I aim to undertake a respectful approach through my actions, as well as through consultation. These actions extend well beyond verbally acknowledging and paying respect to the Traditional Owners and Elders of the Country that I am working on. It means ensuring early engagement, so as to allow time to build a trusting relationship and ensure cultural protocols and decision-making processes of the community can be incorporated into the project timeframe; or alternatively, and better still, to allow it to drive the project timeframe. Often project timeframes are tight, but the earlier the conversation begins to start building this relationship, the greater and more positive the influence will be on the project. Strong everyday relationships are built on informal conversations – this approach is no different. Consider these informal discussions every time, prior to getting down to business. I don't believe there would be many people who would disclose information they held to someone they didn't know and were unsure if they could trust?

Traditional Owner Elders are sought after to provide advice on an enormous range of issues affecting their communities and as there are only a small number of them in any community, we cannot expect them to have an in-depth understanding of what the design profession can offer. We cannot assume the community understands design or technical language, so it's important to use plain English in conversations. At the same time, we need to really listen to what is being spoken – this is often referred to as deep listening. This is not as easy as it sounds. Everyone can hear what someone says, but it takes a different skill—often learnt over many years—to really listen and hear the message behind the spoken words.

Lastly, if the Traditional Owners are bringing their knowledge (being their commodity) to the table, we must ask ourselves, what are we bringing – both personally and professionally? It needs to be more than just the project delivery. Projects are often opportunities for possible employment for communities, but they are just that—opportunities—and they generally only come to fruition in the long term. We need to consider other community benefits as part of the process.

+ Working with Aboriginal communities requires deep listening and continuous reflection. When have you got it wrong and what lessons did this teach you?

AP I have been fortunate enough to live in various locations across Australia, from Far North Queensland to southern Australia and across to the southeast, working with a number of Aboriginal communities. Experiencing the diversity of cultures in these communities made me appreciate that I needed to continue to build on my understandings of what I had learnt from a previous community, not rely on it as a general understanding for all Aboriginal and Torres Strait Islander cultures.

When I first started engaging with Aboriginal communities I did extensive reading about Aboriginal culture and didn't properly appreciate that the information was often written from a non-Aboriginal perspective. I was quickly reminded that Indigenous knowledge was passed down orally and that written accounts don't always capture the true cultural meaning. As I built on my experiences engaging with communities, I continued to gain a deeper understanding of an Aboriginal way of seeing. Speaking, or "yarning" with a community would always leave me much richer for the experience!

+ What recommendations do you have for landscape architects and designers who are at the beginning of building connections with First Peoples?

AP Considering our profession with our direct relationship with the landscape through developing, manipulating, and rehabilitating I continue to find it quite astonishing the number of people that have never met or spoken to an Aboriginal or Torres Strait Islander person. Granted, Aboriginal and Torres Strait Islander people make up only a very small minority at just over 3% of Australia's population, but how can we not seek Indigenous knowledge and understanding of Country to ensure the long-term sustainability of this landscape?

I speak to many people who are concerned that they will say something inappropriate or be misunderstood about their intentions when speaking with Traditional Owners. If you ensure you consider a respectful approach of engaging, then this reduces the chances of misunderstandings. Communities are very attuned to genuine, respectful engagement. Bringing an open mind with a non-presumptive attitude to the conversation will stand you in good stead.

PP The first step in building connections with First Peoples is to ensure you correctly seek out who it is you should be speaking to. If you are interested in engaging the community in a general nature, then reaching out to an Aboriginal organization is a great first step – they will be able to advise on the right people to speak to initially. But if you are interested in building a relationship with a particular community to discuss more site-specific issues, then you really need to speak to the Traditional Owners for the area. Developing a relationship with the Traditional Owners is the first step, but even more important is to continue to build on the relationship – to continue the conversations. True engagement requires a long-term relationship based on trust, respect, and honesty.

Opposite: Graphic recording of the Connection to Country Symposium 2016 by Sarah Firth.

Jos Boys directs the MSc in Learning Environments at The Bartlett, University College London, with a research focus on creative and inclusive educational spaces both within and beyond the academy. She is cofounder, with Zoe Partington, of The DisOrdinary Architecture Project, a platform bringing together disabled artists and built environment students, educators, and practitioners for creative and positive actions and dialogue that can demonstrate how disability is a valuable and generative force in design, rather than a technical and legalistic "problem." As well as several books on learning spaces, Jos is the author of *Doing Disability Differently: An Alternative Handbook on Architecture, Dis/ability, and Designing for Everyday Life* (2014) and editor of *Disability, Space, Architecture: A Reader* (2017).

+ ARCHITECTURE, DISABILITY STUDIES, ART

Concepts like public and community seem pretty straightforward. Anyone can understand what they mean. Who, though, is the public? Notions of "the people as a whole" or of communities that unproblematically share characteristics, attitudes, or interests in common can hide as much as they reveal. Instead we should ask: how are our ordinary conceptual, lived, and built worlds framed by unnoticed assumptions about what "the public" knows and does? What kinds of bodies are valued and validated in these processes, and who is ignored, mis-recognized, marginalized, or misrepresented? What are the everyday, unnoticed social, material, aesthetic, and spatial practices that perpetuate one particular normality over others? How do such processes of normalization work? And how can "normal" practices be resisted, challenged, or remade when they act normatively–that is, inequitably–on some people rather than others, making invisible certain knowledges and experiences, and enabling some bodies, whilst disabling others?

This requires that we first take better critical notice of situations where someone is simultaneously assumed to be part of the public or a community, but is also not: what Titchkosky calls "included as excludable."[1] How public is a space if you cannot access it? Who is part of a community that bonds around common-sense practices that treat some others (women, people of color, queer and trans people) as inherently inferior? Crucially, we need to see that experiences of exclusion are not individual anomalies, matters that can be rectified on a case-by-case basis through design or social intervention. The framing of everyday social and spatial practices for "people in general" obscures its inherent but unspoken patterning of who is allowed in and who is left out. In his paper "On Doing 'Being Ordinary,'" Harvey Sacks proposes that partaking in everyday life is a kind of work that constantly remakes what is normal in our encounters, through the multitude of behavioral, social, aesthetic, material, and spatial cues that have to be recognized and then continually (re)produced.[2] But this work acts differentially:

> So one part of the job [doing "being ordinary"] is that you have to know what anybody/ everybody is doing: doing ordinarily. Further, you have to have that available to do. There are people who do not have that available to do, and who specifically cannot be ordinary.[3]

George Payne gives a simple example of such cues:

> "Anyone" knows how to sit down. Generally no one asks permission to sit down. Anyone does it and knows how to do it. However, what anyone also knows is that in some circumstances some people have to wait to be seated, stand in a queue, wait until a table is available, wait until the judge has sat down and so on. In particular cases, people are marked down to acquire an identity, which sets them apart from "anyone."[4]

Being marked and set apart makes you the misfit. Someone with a disability for whom sitting down may not be straightforward can find themselves no longer just "anyone," rather they may become over-visible in being seen to breach normal everyday actions. Of course, who sits and where they sit is complicated and nuanced, intersected both by embodied differences and by the "normal" practices of the particular space in which they find themselves. A person of color may be assumed to be in the wrong place or a woman may be expected to sit in a certain way. There is a way to sit and behave in a public lecture[5] and a way to sit on a museum bench.[6]

How, then, does this intersect with designing public spaces? A particular type of user–a particular anyone–may be explicitly articulated by the designer or they may be just assumed. They may be contested or ignored or absent-mindedly transformed through

Previous: Learning to "breach" – experiencing space as an encumbered person.

Opposite: An elderly woman repurposes a bike rack as a seat.

actions by the client, contractor, or others. So our assumptions about anyone are always being translated (unevenly) into social, aesthetic, material, and spatial landscapes. However, buildings and public spaces are still predominantly designed for an anyone who is able-bodied, whilst meeting disabled people's multiple requirements and desires becomes merely a functional and legalistic add-on to meet requirements or notions of accessibility at the end of the design process. This is what Jay Dolmage calls retrofitting.[7]

We need to ask instead how disability comes to be framed as an atheoretical, non-historical concept, with the diverse constituencies of disabled people predominantly framed as a problem, precisely because they appear not to "fit" with normal design processes. Simultaneously we need to ask why and how able bodies can continue to have the privilege of assuming themselves as an unproblematic and obvious anyone.[8] Through the DisOrdinary Architecture Project[9]–a UK-based platform led by disabled artists–we have been exploring critical and creative ways of challenging such unnoticed and common-sense framings, by developing alternative ways of working for built environment education and practice. Co-founded by artist Zoe Partington and me, this is a platform bringing together disabled artists and built environment students, educators, and practitioners for collaborative dialogue, experiments, and design interventions that aim to demonstrate how disability is in fact a valuable and generative force in design, rather than a technical and legalistic "problem." DisOrdinary Architecture's mission is "to promote activity that develops and captures models of new practice for the built environment, led by the creativity and experiences of disabled artists." The group, in various iterations, has been building its expertise in codeveloping dis/ability and architectural activities since 2008. It has a committed network of about 15 disabled artists, together with a larger group who get involved in particular projects, as well as a similar number of architectural students, educators, and professionals who support the work.

The DisOrdinary Architecture Project makes three big claims. First, we believe in starting from difference – valuing the richness of our bio- and neuro-diversity and our many different ways of being in the world, rather than relying on norms, "anyone," or average users. We want to show how engaging with the experiences and expertise of what are often called unruly or non-compliant bodies is both powerful and enjoyable. Second, we argue that investigating dis/ability (and other forms of difference) opens up a vital critique of normative practices and spaces. Third, we challenge how "retrofitting" and current accessibility design guidance perpetuates ability/disability oppositional binaries in built space, to the detriment of everyone. Informed by important work by disabled artists, activists, and scholars, we explore how dis/ability can be reframed, not as a simplistic binary, but as a complex, intersectional, situated and dynamic patterning of enabling

and disabling practices and spaces. This means there are no simplistic design solutions that can be mindlessly applied (as currently often happens through when designers rely on compliance with building codes). Instead, we need to start codeveloping collective and emergent design practices led by disabled and other disadvantaged people's experiences and expertise, which looks for shared affinities, but also accepts tensions and contradictions in how diverse people can be enabled by the design of built space.[10]

Our various activities to date across built environment education and practice internationally include developmental workshops; artistic and design experiments and provocations; explorations of alternative design methods, representations, and guidance; and research and consultancy with built environment professionals on design projects. The ultimate aim is to change mindsets and cultures by developing a rich and expanding compendium of ideas, strategies, and tactics for (re)thinking and (re)doing design that can go beyond the frustrating limitations of the current relationship of building and spatial design to disability, structured through compliance (regulations and design guidance) and underpinned by commonplace social, material, aesthetic, and spatial practices that keeps disability in its "place." I will outline three aspects of what we do to give a flavor of what such a program suggests. This is still work in progress – small steps that we hope will snowball toward real change in how dis/ability and design intersect.

First, we have been exploring how to both challenge and reformulate everyday concepts and terminologies that frame disability–both in everyday life and in built environment disciplines' approaches and methods–in ways that disabled people themselves often don't recognize.[11] For example, the very notion of access and inclusion assumes a normal to which non-normals should be allowed entry, without challenging what constitutes the normal in the first place, merely increasing its diversity. Notions of accessibility can therefore depoliticize and neutralize inequality and discrimination, sliding away from real underlying issues of social, material, and spatial justice. Sara Ahmed has shown how a similar framing works to contain people of color, by also making the problem of exclusion remain with the marginalized groups that it affects:

> It is certainly the case that responsibility for diversity and equality is unevenly distributed. It is also the case that the distribution of this work is political: if diversity and equality work is less valued by organizations, then to become responsible for this work can mean to inhabit institutional spaces that are also less valued.[12]

In this process the white able body is absolved of responsibility for reproducing differential access to, and engagement with, built space. Similarly, the notion of "having empathy with" people with disabilities acts to center the positive change on the non-disabled person (they can feel better about themselves) rather than, for example, terms like advocacy or being an ally that require supporting actions. To combat these ideas, DisOrdinary Architecture uses concepts of fitting and misfitting, as articulated by disability studies scholar Rosemarie Garland Thomson:

> A sustaining environment is a material context of received and built things ranging from accessibly designed public spaces, welcoming natural surroundings, communication devices, tools, and implements, as well as other people. A fit occurs when a harmonious, proper interaction occurs between a particularly shaped and functioning body and an environment that sustains that body. A misfit occurs when the environment does not sustain the shape and function of the body that enters it. The dynamism between body and world that produces fits or misfits comes at the spatial and temporal points of encounter between dynamic but relatively stable bodies and environments. The built and arranged space through which we navigate our lives tends to offer fits to majority bodies and create misfits with minority forms of embodiment, such as people with disabilities.[13]

Using fitting/misfitting rather than abled/disabled has many advantages. It is inherently relational (it always depends on particular encounters and contexts). Almost everyone is likely to have experienced misfitting in some situations. What is more, it makes "fitting" equally problematic. To fit smoothly into this world means not needing to notice everyday encounters with objects, spaces, and others; that is, being able to just run up some stairs, or ignore a noisy place or flickering light, or walk unthinkingly across a slippery or uneven surface. To find you misfit (because of diverse bio- and neuro-variations, within specific social encounters or environments) is frustrating, exhausting, often time-consuming, and demeaning, but it also produces very creative negotiations with others and built space. Paying close attention to, and mapping, mis/fitting across built landscapes can be a creative tool for unraveling both how space acts differentially to enable some bodies and disable others, and for better understanding how "unruly" bodies find creative ways of making spaces work better (what some disabled people call life hacks).[14] For example, I recently saw an older woman sitting on a cycle rack frame. This necessary act (to find somewhere to sit down in public)–where sitting is framed in specific acceptable ways and often infrequently provided–challenges just who "anyone" is in public space. It demonstrates both her creativity in unsupportive circumstances, and what she is not – the fit, mobile, unencumbered, and able body, whose accessibility is increased through the provision of public bicycle-related facilities. And her act raises more than its individual case. Political and design support for cycling is a current priority in many cities whereas, for example, public toilets are not. The focus on cycling as a means of improving health and wellbeing makes invisible an alternative – that accessible public restrooms also hugely benefit the health of many people, particularly those who are already less able to access the public realm. Thus is public space shaped to enable particular bodies and not others.

A second aspect of what the DisOrdinary Architecture Project does is to rethink and reshape design discourses, approaches, methods, and forms of representation across education and practice. This includes various foundational exercises that ask students, educators, and professionals to explore what makes an embodied design practice (that is, what our body-minds can bring to our experiences and actions within the discipline). This can involve, for example, forms of performative, narrative, and investigative drawing that experiment with positively reshaping bodies and their interrelationships to each other and to material space. It can inform ways of learning history and theory, or engaging with technologies. It intersects in fascinating ways with, for example, sustainability and post-humanism.[15] We explore design methods that go beyond the limitations of what orthography can capture, to express multiple embodied experiences through audio-description, tactile sketching, sensory mapping, and modeling.[16] This also involves rethinking how bodies can be more variously represented in designers' work.[17]

We are particularly interested in using a technique called breaching to unravel normative elements in everyday social and spatial practices. Breaching is a method of deliberately not acting normally in various contexts, to open up the intricate details of how social and spatial norms work. One form of breaching is to take on characteristics of a misfitting body, for example, by moving through space differently, or performing unexpected actions.[18] Another is to experiment with altering aspects of "ordinary" social and spatial practices, as a creative generator for design. Partially sighted artist Zoe Partington has developed character scenarios that ask participants to undertake actions such as carrying unwieldy loads, walking very slowly or in redefined patterns, to capture and analyze different kinds of relationships to space.

A third aspect is in developing design processes, strategies, and interventions that can make an immediate impact on existing design practice and on the production of built landscapes. We have emerging projects exploring different kinds of design manifestos, as well as creative and multi-layered alternatives to existing banal, compliance-driven design guidance. We are working with a number of practices on participatory design processes that use codesigning workshops to bring together disabled artists and other stakeholders at key moments in design development. We are exploring how ideas of multimodality[18] could suggest design possibilities that value

1 Tanya Titchkosky, *The Question of Access: Disability, Space, Meaning* (University of Toronto Press, 2011). See also Tanya Titchkosky, "The Educated Sensorium and the Inclusion of Disabled People as Excludable," *Scandinavian Journal of Disability Research*, 21 no. 1 (2019): 282–90.

2 Harvey Sacks, "On doing 'being ordinary,'" in J. Atkinson (ed.), *Structures of Social Action* (Cambridge University Press, 1985), 413–29.

3 Ibid., 415.

4 G.C. Payne, "Making a Lesson Happen: an ethnomethodolgical analysis," in M. Hammersley & P. Woods (eds), *The Process of Schooling* (Routledge, 1976), 33.

5 Aaron Williamson, "The Collapsing Lecture," in Jos Boys (ed.) *Disability, Space, Architecture: A Reader* (Routledge, 2017), 173–82.

6 Diana Fuss & Joel Sanders, "An Aesthetic Headache: Notes from the Museum Bench," in Johanna Burton, Lynne Cooke & Josiah McElheny (eds) *Interiors* (Sternberg Press, 2012), 67.

7 Jay Dolmage, "From Steep Steps to Retrofit to Universal Design, from Collapse to Austerity," in *Disability, Space, Architecture*, ibid., 102–14. Dolmage writes that to "retrofit is to add a component or accessory to something that has been already manufactured or built. This retrofit does not necessarily make the product function better, does not necessarily fix a faulty product, but it acts as a sort of correction – it adds a modernized part in place of, or in addition to, an older part... (It) is a sort of cure, but half-hearted, thus leaving many people with disabilities in difficult positions."

8 "As language recommends that we conceive of the able-body as something that just comes along 'naturally' as people go about their daily existence...All of this glosses the body that comes along while, at the same time, brings it along metaphorically. Speaking of 'normal bodies' as movement and metaphor maps them as if they are a natural possession, as if they are not mapped at all." Tanya Titchkosky, "Cultural Maps: Which way to disability?" in Miriam Corker & Tom Shakespeare (eds), *Disability/Postmodernity: Embodying Disability Theory* (Continuum, 2002), 103.

9 For more details go to www.disordinaryarchitecture.co.uk. For videos about our work see https://vimeo.com/showcase/4562223.

10 See, for example, *Access is Love* by the Disability Visibility Project and Aimi Hamraie's *Mapping Access* work at the University of Vanderbilt.

11 I explore this in greater depth in chapter one "Challenging Common Sense" in *Doing Disability Differently: An alternative handbook on architecture, dis/ability and designing for everyday life* (Routledge, 2014), 11–22.

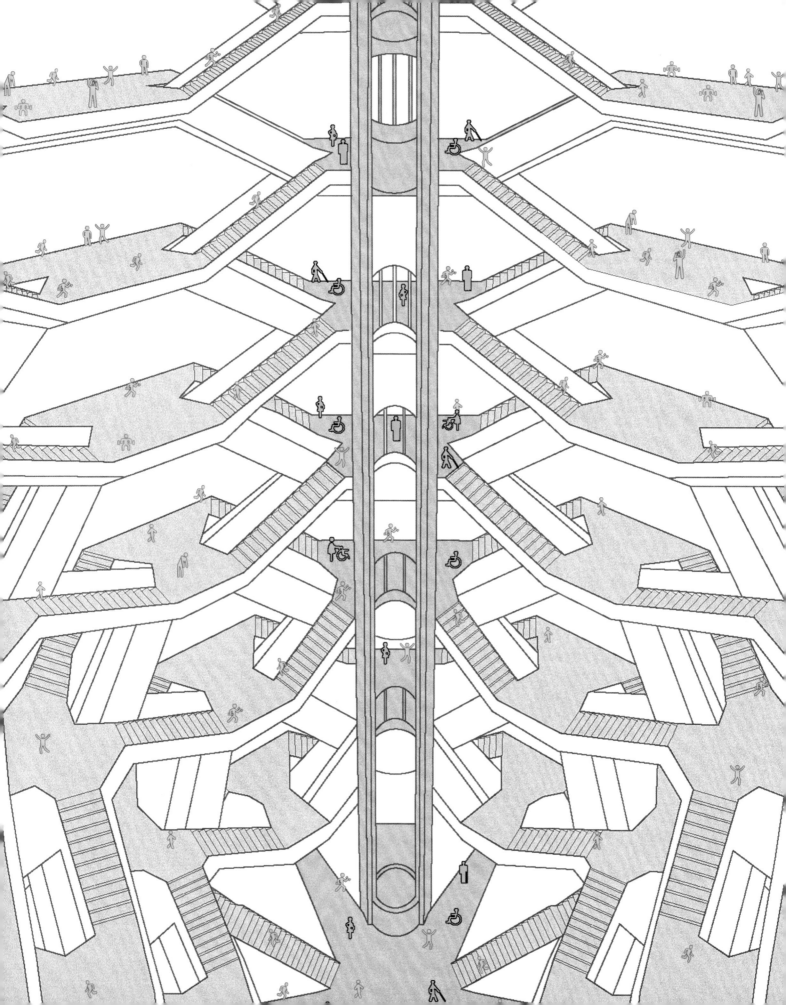

and enable multiple ways of being in the world, through offering many varieties of spatial and social relationships layered across a built space.

Recently, the owners of Vessel, a public attraction built as part of the Hudson Yards development in New York and designed by Heatherwick Studios, were threatened with legal action by the US Department of Justice regarding the attraction's failure to provide for accessibility by individuals with disabilities. By agreement, a new platform lift mechanism will now be installed on the upper levels of Vessel to enable disabled people to enjoy the views from the top, previously only accessible to the (very) able-bodied. Vessel's current design allows individuals with disabilities to access at most only three of the 80 platforms, using one, often very busy, public elevator. This was only after some creative campaigning under the banner of the Anti-Stairs Club Lounge, coordinated by disabled artist Shannon Finnigan.[19]

I want to end by arguing that this should not be dismissed as just a problem for this specific case and its clients and designers. It is not about blame. What it does is expose the tensions between the assumed values of concept-driven design and the presumed restrictions on creativity of ADA compliance. Such a false dichotomy underpins most design, not just this example. Like public investment in cycling, it is also framed by particular mindsets—both popularly and across the built environment disciplines—that continue to be based on an anyone (or "public in general") who is mobile, energetic, unencumbered, and fit, and who, in the public realm, will "obviously" enjoy consuming spectacular sensory experiences that enhance the experience of living in that kind of body. But what if we thought and designed differently, if we started from difference and from taking notice of, and engaging with, multi-modal ways of getting around a space? Working with misfits, outliers, and unruly bodies has the potential to generate multi-layered and exciting design opportunities, not to be merely a boring limitation on design imaginations. Imagine Vessel (and other similar spectacular public spaces) as a means for many diverse people to circulate—in this case upwards—to enhance our many various ways of being in the world; to choose to move both easily or with effort, to sit and watch or to move around, to see the view and to feel the wind on your face. Only when we can design for such variety from the start, can we be making truly equitable (and beautiful) spaces.

12 Sara Ahmed, *On Being Included: Racism and Diversity in Institutional Life* (Duke University Press, 2012), 4.

13 Rosemarie Garland-Thomson, "The Story of My Work: How I Became Disabled," *DSQ: Disability Studies Quarterly* 34, no. 2 (2014).

14 See, for example, disabled artist Rachel Gadsden with Judit Pusztaszeri and students from the University of Brighton UK, "Narratives of Difference," https://vimeo.com/321870384 and disabled artist Liz Crow with Julia Dwyer and students from the University of Westminster UK, "Tilted Horizons," https://vimeo.com/showcase/4562223/video/215407274.

15 For an overview, see "Starting from Difference," https://vimeo.com/showcase/4562223/video/295201185.

16 See, for example, the "Architecture Beyond Sight" project, a collaboration between The Bartlett UCL and the DisOrdinary Architecture Project: collaborative development video, https://vimeo.com/296974975; film by Anna Ulrike Andersen, https://vimeo.com/user6262581; blind and partially sighted participants' blogs, Fae Kilburn https://disabilityarts.online/blog/fae-kilburn/architecture-beyond-sight/ and Clarke Reynolds https://outsidein.org.uk/news/dis-ordinary-architecture-a-visionary-course/.

17 See the work of Thomas Carpentier, "The New Standard," https://www.thomascarpentier.com/The-New-Standard, and Sophie Handler, *Public Seating. Resistant Sitting: The Pensioner's Alternative Street Furniture Guide Project Report* (RIBA/Ice McAslan Bursary, 2009) and *An Alternative Age-Friendly Handbook* (The University of Manchester Library, 2014), https://www.architecture.com/knowledge-and-resources/resources-landing-page/age-friendly-handbook.

18 Melanie Yergeau et al., "Multimodality in Motion: Disability and Kairotic Spaces," in *Kairos: A Journal of Rhetoric, Technology, and Pedagogy*, 18, no. 1 (2013).

19 For perspectives on Vessel from disability activism, scholarship, and arts see Sam Berman, "The Vessel: Is NYC's Newest Landmark Accessible to All?" https://equalentry.com/the-vessel-is-nycs-newest-landmark-accessible-for-all/; Kevin Gotkin, "Stair Worship: Heatherwick's Vessel," *The Avery Review*, https://www.averyreview.com/issues/33/stair-worship; Emily Sara, "Fighting the Art World's Ableism," (August 2, 2019), https://hyperallergic.com/510439/fighting-the-art-worlds-ableism/.

Opposite: Heatherwick Studios' Vessel project in New York was required to be retrofitted to improve access for individuals with disabilities.

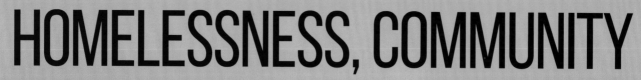

HOMELESSNESS, COMMUNITY

AND HOSTILE ARCHITECTURE

JAMES PETTY + ALISON YOUNG

Melbourne is Australia's second largest city. From 2011 to 2017 Melbourne was ranked by The Economist as "the world's most livable city."[1] This was despite also being ranked one of the least affordable cities in the world during the same period.[2] In 2016, a group of homeless people established a camp in Melbourne's central business district to protest the chronic lack of affordable housing. They set up camp around a tree in a small square on Elizabeth Street, the city's main thoroughfare. In response, the then-Lord Mayor said, "Everybody has the right to protest but that doesn't give you the right to camp."[3]

After three weeks, officers of the Melbourne City Council dismantled the camp. Most of the protestors moved to another, less central, park. Overnight, large flowerbeds in heavy steel and concrete planters were installed where the camp had been. To passers-by and those unaware of the protest, the flowerbeds appear decorative – just another ornament in the world's most livable city. To the protestors, they were a coercive mechanism that automated their exclusion from the space.

James Petty is an honorary research fellow in criminology at the University of Melbourne. His research interests include homelessness and housing, urban design and public space, alcohol and other drugs, and marginalized populations. His PhD thesis investigated the criminalization of homelessness in Melbourne.

Alison Young is the Francine V. McNiff Professor of Criminology at the University of Melbourne, Australia. She is currently researching ride-sharing and public safety (with Bianca Fileborn and Elena Cama), homelessness and public space (with James Petty), and the atmospherics of criminal justice institutions. She is author of eight books including *Street Art World* (2016), *Street Art, Public City* (2014), *The Scene of Violence* (2010), and *Street/Studio* (2010).

+ URBAN DESIGN, SOCIOLOGY, CRIMINOLOGY

There are two main ways for a community to define itself. The first is to identify what binds members of the community – the shared values, beliefs, and standards; and the second is to identify the boundary of the community – the line that separates those who belong ("us") from those who do not ("them"). While the first approach is arguably more rewarding, the easiest way to establish and maintain a community boundary is to identify those on the other side of it: outlaws, criminals, strangers, "Others." Those who are visibly homeless inhabit an uncertain position in relation to community boundaries. They often occupy the shared spaces of a community; however, they are unlikely to conform to the norms of that community (such as being housed). Whether homeless people "belong" to a community or not becomes a highly vexed question.

It is not surprising, then, that many communities—and the local government authorities that represent them—struggle to respond to homelessness. The real causes of homelessness—complex interactions of arbitrary forces like inflation, interest rates, unemployment, debt-to-GDP ratio, and a lack of adequate welfare infrastructure—are well beyond the sphere of influence for local governments, yet despite this, there is an enduring expectation of local governments to respond to issues of homelessness within their communities.

Over the last two decades, levels of homelessness have increased in many places around the world. Cities in Australia, the UK, the US, Canada, and other countries have experienced highly public contests around homelessness and what to do about it. An internet search yields numerous examples: police in Florida arrest a 90-year-old man for handing out meals to homeless people; unending debates about Toronto's Downtown East Side; coercive "sweeps" of homeless camps by police and city officials in Seattle; the introduction of bans on various behaviors in Palo Alto, Manchester, Toronto – the list goes on. These contests over visible homelessness are often long and drawn out. In the last decade, many such contests have come to a head in cities such as Melbourne, Sydney, Seattle, London, Berkeley, Las Vegas, Budapest, and others. The results are often punitive "crackdowns" on homelessness and the introduction of laws and regulations prohibiting various behaviors associated with homelessness: camping, begging, sitting on sidewalks, sleeping in a car, public urination, and so on.

In 2014, a photograph of metal spikes installed on the floor of an alcove by the entrance to a high-end apartment building in South London circulated on Twitter. Making international headlines, the tweet introduced the term "hostile architecture" to the public consciousness. Following public outcry, including condemnation by London's then-Mayor Boris Johnson, the spikes were removed (a large pot plant appeared in their place).[4] More so than other forms of coercion, hostile architecture–the use of the built environment to render space unusable by a select group–seems to capture the dystopian imaginary. While the homeless, displaced, and indigent have been subject to other forms of coercion for centuries, the "built-in-ness" of hostile architecture is seen as emblematic of social inequality. High-profile examples, such as the spikes in London, are able to convert public indifference into outrage.

Recent contests over homeless people's inhabitation of public space have felt distinctly contemporary – as though these issues are unique to the present moment. However, homelessness has always been a challenge for cities. Housing is the primary organizational premise of cities and, in consequence, urban environments are shaped by an expectation that inhabitants are housed. This, in turn, carries a series of expectations and norms about people's appearance, behavior, and movement within urban spaces. The visible presence of homeless people disrupts these norms, often evoking an atmosphere of disorder, even danger, for other inhabitants or visitors.

In the 1970s, architect and city planner Oscar Newman developed and championed defensible space theory. In short, Newman proposed that by altering how shared spaces are designed–for example, the forecourts of community housing estates–you can cultivate a sense of communal ownership and responsibility, changing how residents relate to the space and one another.[5] This idea makes sense: if people value a space, they are likely to spend time there and invest in its maintenance. By increasing natural surveillance and opportunities for social interaction while decreasing unused space, a more cohesive community is fostered. In turn, this reduces localized criminal offending and the "decay" of shared spaces. Newman's theory was widely, if unevenly, implemented in the US before falling out of favor in the 1980s.

Since then, the basis of Newman's theory has become somewhat twisted. Predicated on a narrow definition of community membership, the sense of ownership now fostered is achieved via the identification and exclusion of those perceived as "Others": the homeless, drug users, criminals, and so on. The original emphasis on *designing in* positive and inclusive community declined into a focus on *designing out* those elements viewed negatively. As a result, today few spaces are built to support positive social interactions between community members. Domestic residences are designed with security in mind (to keep out the unwanted and dangerous) and public spaces to facilitate sanctioned forms of consumption (i.e., shopping). Community is replaced with (safe) consumerism and the spaces and the methods for regulating them come to reflect this.

A prime example of this shift away from genuinely communal spaces is public seating. Significant decreases in accessible seating have been documented in many cities. What little remains is either reserved for those wealthy enough to access it (e.g., outdoor seating at a café) or is designed to actively prevent uses other than sitting for a short time. This gradual shift poses the question what happens to those unable to adhere to the social, spatial, and behavioral norms of urban spaces? And what happens to those unable to shop, or those who need somewhere to sit for longer, or to lie down to sleep?

There is often a tragic irony to the designing out of homelessness in a particular area. In many cases, the homeless are the long-term inhabitants while those complaining about the homeless are recent, and arriving hard on the heels of gentrification. Fitzroy, an inner-city suburb of Melbourne is a useful example. Once labeled a "slum," historically Fitzroy has nourished a highly diverse community – the homeless, injecting drug users, migrants, artists, the working poor, and others. Gentrification has priced these groups out and the suburb's population has gradually homogenized. However, because of its history, many charities and social services are concentrated in the suburb. Now, the disadvantaged clients of these services must travel to Fitzroy from other, less desirable, areas to access them. This to-and-fro fuels conflict between the homeless, newer residents, and local authorities. Other cities have their own versions of this same pattern: new developments push out the poor and disenfranchised to make way for increased economic flows; new residents feel threatened by the original inhabitants of the area, which precipitates new and often punitive strategies to deal with them.

While some vulnerable groups are able to successfully transition to new areas, others are less well-equipped. The visibly homeless–at the extreme edge of vulnerability– are one such group. They often rely on areas with high foot traffic to earn their living. Boulevards, tourist hotspots, and entertainment precincts are an obvious choice. Commonly, it is claims about the economic impacts of homelessness (for example, on tourism) that precipitate regulatory changes. Of course, being homeless is not illegal. Formally criminalizing homelessness would strike against many of the founding principles of Western democracy and other systems of statehood. Further, while the public is not necessarily fond of visible homelessness, they may not stand for explicit state violence against the poor and vulnerable.[6] As a result, regulatory authorities often seek workarounds banning specific behaviors associated with homelessness such as begging, loitering, panhandling, and sleeping in public. Such laws are often accompanied by the specious justification that the homed and wealthy aren't allowed to beg either. However, one weakness of new regulations is that they require enforcement, and therefore resources and time. Hostile architecture offers something of a solution to this problem.

While some examples of hostile architecture lack subtlety (e.g., park benches with retractable coin-operated spikes,[7] and pink overhead lighting to discourage teenagers from congregating in certain areas),[8] lessons are learnt quickly. Hostile design can be easily hidden within the broader aesthetics of public amenity: garden beds, street sculptures, curved public seating, and "artistically" gradated surfaces. Even public infrastructure itself can be deployed to hostile purposes. In 2017, a group of homeless people encamped at one of Melbourne's main train stations during the Australian Open – an international tennis tournament drawing many tourists. After significant public outcry, fueled by the tabloid media, the camp and campers were forcibly removed. Scaffolding was erected around the station's façade blocking off the area where the protestors had camped. Officially, the scaffolding was for planned renovation

works; however, it remained in place for more than a year before any work began. In Perth, Australia, a state government department installed high-powered water jets in the building's courtyard where homeless people often slept at night. These would activate periodically, soaking the area and anyone who was sleeping there. This demonstrates how hostile architecture can be installed in such a way so as to only be apparent to those it directly impacts.

While not every example is as subtle as garden beds or scaffolding, it is becoming more difficult to measure the uptake and prevalence of hostile architecture. In many cities, there is a convergence of hostile design and public amenity. In Seattle, for example, public bike racks were installed beneath a bridge where homeless people often camped. The area was not near a cycling track nor popular with cyclists, yet it is now absent of the homeless. Hostile architecture is an invisible war waged in public space.

The widespread adoption of hostile architecture by city councils and other bodies, and the acceptance of this by local communities, points to two things. First, a decreasing public tolerance for visible homelessness and, second, a desire for more aggressively curated public space. It is difficult to pinpoint a time when urban and spatial design departed from the concept of inclusivity so decisively. Certainly, it can be linked to what criminologists refer to as the "punitive turn" – a shift in governmental thinking away from ideals like rehabilitation and social justice in favor of harsh, punitive responses.

Generally, the punitive turn refers to changes in criminal justice – mandatory minimum sentencing and three-strikes laws. However, this thinking also impacts social services. Homelessness, once considered a problem *of* society became viewed as a problem *for* society. This shift can be further contextualized in relation to the rise of a new individualism borne from the politics of the 1980s – exemplified by UK Prime Minister Margaret Thatcher's dark claim, "There is no such thing as society." In some ways, the decade was the nail in the coffin of communitarian thought – notions of social well-being and "the greater good" gave way to a new focus on the individual. Social problems like homelessness became understood solely in relation to their impact on the consumer-citizen. Considerations of the social good were, like the homeless themselves, banished to the margins.

We describe this change in how public spaces are managed as a shift from ethics to aesthetics. The exemplary characteristic of this is no longer viewing built environments as a social resource but as financial assets reserved exclusively for wealthy consumers. These spaces, which in many cities make up most of the urban space, are premised on the exclusion of others. As such, these spaces and those who spend time in them are always threatened by the presence of those who appear "out of place." The use of the built environment to control inhabitants is not new: footpaths determine where we walk, traffic lights regulate when and where we cross the road, squares define where we congregate and mingle, and so on. Michel de Certeau knew this when he looked down at New York City from the viewing platform of the World Trade Center.[9] However, hostile architecture is a step beyond mere orchestration. The examples highlighted here indicate how public space is being weaponized against the vulnerable.

We argue that the increasing deployment of hostile architecture indicates several things. First, the failure to effectively advocate for systemic solutions to homelessness and other social problems. Second, a shift from ethics to aesthetics in how urban environments are managed and regulated. And third, a public acceptance of the fallacy that widespread homelessness is inevitable and therefore best dealt with cheaply and harshly.

The most frustrating thing about this is that effective solutions to problems like homelessness do exist. While the causes of homelessness are complex, the factors that protect against it are well understood. Public housing, security of tenure, financial literacy, accessible social services, social connection, and adequate welfare, all have strong protective functions against homelessness. In fact, an Australian study found that the most important factor determining whether someone becomes homeless or not is the availability of public housing.[10]

While most governments are reluctant to adopt system-wide changes, some have. Utah in the US and Wales in the UK have adopted housing policies that have quickly and effectively reduced the levels of systemic homelessness over the long-term. These programs save millions in downstream costs, as well as reducing the widespread social harms associated with homelessness. Hostile architecture is viewed as a simpler and cheaper option. However, at best, hostile architecture hides or displaces visible poverty. At worst, it makes an already harsh environment harsher still for those forced to inhabit it. Further, in the absence of effective, evidence-based responses to homelessness, the social harms associated with it increase and compound. Long-term and systemic responses are more complex and require more up-front funding. However, arguably the most difficult part is challenging the currently narrow conceptions of community. Arming the edges between one group of community members and another with hostile architecture is not a path forward, nor does it offer lasting or meaningful solutions.

Community has never meant homogeneity. People experiencing homelessness are members of our communities whether we like it or not. The homeless are not a discrete population that can be effectively excised. With inadequate and piecemeal welfare, new people enter into homelessness every day. Without ongoing systemic solutions, they will continue to use the spaces that are available to them. Hostile architecture offers a false promise of a world where homeless people are somewhere else, hidden from view. Surely a better alternative is a world where no one is forced to sleep on the streets.

1 Wendall Cox, Hugh Pavletich & Oliver Hartwich, *13th Annual Demographia International Housing Affordability Survey* (2017), http://demographia.com/dhi.pdf.

2 Demographia, *Annual Demographia International Housing Affordability Survey*, (2011–2017) Performance Urban Planning: Belleville, Illinois, USA.

3 Benjamin Priess, Liam Mannix & Clay Lucas, "Thieves and addicts force City Square homeless camp to split," *The Age* (18 May 2016), https://www.theage.com.au/national/victoria/eviction-looming-for-homeless-protesters-in-city-square-20160518-goxwjo.html.

4 Ben Quinn, "Anti-homeless Spikes are Part of a Wider Phenomenon of Hostile Architecture," *The Guardian* (June 13, 2014), https://www.theguardian.com/artanddesign/2014/jun/13/anti-homeless-spikes-hostile-architecture.

5 Oscar Newman, *Defensible Space: Crime Prevention through Urban Design* (MacMillan, 1972).

6 Charles Baudelaire, *The Madness of the Day*, trans. Lydia Davis (Station Hill Press, 1981).

7 "Pay and Sit: the First Coin-Operated Park Bench," *Techeblog*, https://www.techeblog.com/pay-and-sit-the-first-coin-operated-park-bench/.

8 Pink neon lighting was used by one local council in the UK to deter teenagers from congregating in underpasses at night. The logic was that the pink lighting would highlight the teens' pimples.

9 Michel de Certeau, *The Practice of Everyday Life* (University of California Press, 1984).

10 Guy Johnson, et al., *Journey Home: Findings from Waves 1 to 4* (University of Melbourne Press, 2014).

IN PLACE OVER

ANNE WHISTON SPIRN

Anne Whiston Spirn is the Cecil and Ida Green Distinguished Professor of Landscape Architecture and Planning at MIT. Her books include *The Granite Garden* (1984), *The Language of Landscape* (1998), *Daring to Look* (2008), and *The Eye is a Door* (2014). This essay is an excerpt from her forthcoming book *The Buried River*. Spirn received Japan's 2001 International Cosmos Prize for "contributions to the harmonious coexistence of nature and mankind" and the 2018 National Design Award for "Design Mind."

✛ LANDSCAPE ARCHITECTURE, HYDROLOGY

PHILADELPHIA

Mill Creek neighborhood
Mill Creek watershed

In 1987 I would not have predicted that, more than three decades later, I would still be engaged with West Philadelphia's Mill Creek watershed and community. Initially, I did not intend to have a long-term relationship with this place. It started as a four-year, action research and community service project, with the expectation that I would turn over my findings and recommendations to the Philadelphia City Planning Commission, and that the "official" planners would take them on board in their 1994 Plan for West Philadelphia. But, they didn't. Outraged and perplexed, I determined to persist, which led, over the years, to deeper and deeper relationships with the place and its people. What began as research driven by my own goals, grew into a program of mutual teaching and learning with children and adults in the Mill Creek community.

In 1986 I moved to Philadelphia from Boston, where I had been studying urban vacant land as an opportunity both to restore the urban natural environment and to rebuild inner-city communities. There, I discovered a correlation between the buried floodplain of former streams and large tracts of vacant land and envisioned a potential solution to Boston's most pressing environmental problem, the pollution of Boston Harbor by combined sewer overflows (CSOs). Boston, like Philadelphia and many older cities, has combined sanitary and storm sewers, so, after a rainstorm, torrents of sewage rushed into rivers and harbor. Billions of dollars would be spent to build an enormous plant to treat combined sewage from the Boston metropolitan region. I proposed an alternative: prevent stormwater from entering the sewer system in the first place by employing "green" infrastructure to detain or retain runoff. Vacant land in the valley bottoms of inner-city communities could be transformed into parks, their construction and maintenance paid for by funds for water infrastructure. I cited as precedents Frederick Law Olmsted's designs for Boston's Fens and Riverway in the late 19th century. My proposal received a lot of attention, but Boston

TIME
A CASE FOR LONGITUDINAL ACTION RESEARCH

decided to build a new sewage treatment plant instead. When I moved to Philadelphia I knew that, at some point, the federal Clean Water Act would force Philadelphia to deal with pollution from CSOs, and I hoped to persuade the city to adopt the approach I had advocated for in Boston.

At the University of Pennsylvania, I joined with colleagues at Penn and Philadelphia Green in a proposal to the Pew Charitable Trust for funding to "green" West Philadelphia through the design and construction of community gardens. With an eye to extending the Boston research, I persuaded the others to enlarge the project's scope from community gardens to the restoration of the natural environment at large. I was particularly interested in the Mill Creek watershed, which comprised about half of our study area. Mill Creek is a watershed that was drastically reshaped as it was densely urbanized, a river buried in a sewer, and a neighborhood with severe poverty. The correlation between vacant land and the buried stream was clear in the Mill Creek neighborhood. How do you restore the urban natural environment in such places at the same time as rebuilding those neighborhoods, and do so in synergistic ways? My work in Mill Creek would explore how this might be accomplished.

Our work during the first summer of 1987 went against the norms of "proper" research practice, an orderly progression from data collection and analysis, to a synthetic plan for the future and identification of the character and location of design experiments, to detailed design. Instead we were immediately thrown into designing and building community gardens. The process felt upside down, the designs uninformed by research. The design "cases" were not chosen as representative of particular conditions, nor were their locations deliberately selected as strategic; they were vacant lots where neighbors wanted a garden. After a few months, however, I realized what

rich insights this mixed-up process had yielded. Building a project was not the end point. It was a beginning that revealed misleading or overlooked data. The process of bringing a project to fruition and reflecting on the result also generated ideas for an approach to planning as a framework for action, where all citizens, groups, and agencies have a role to play. From then on data collection and analysis, planning, design, and construction, all proceeded apace, each activity informing the others.

The community garden, as it turned out, was a microcosm of community that offered lessons for designing the neighborhood and city. "This garden is a town," Hayward Ford, president of Aspen Farms Community Garden in Mill Creek, told us, "we have everything but a penal colony." The garden's plots were laid out in a grid, each individual territory bordered by paths, like streets. There was a common infrastructure: a drip irrigation system and a compost pile. But, "It isn't all 50 beds of roses," Ford said. There are 50 different people with 50 different ways of seeing things and 50 different ways of doing things. And everybody, of course, is always right." To adjudicate these differences, the gardeners elected leaders and voted on contentious issues. Like pioneers, community gardeners who settle a vacant lot must decide how to govern themselves and how to lay out the garden, and its form reflects its political structure. The grid of plots at Aspen Farms, for example, reflected its democratic organization. We also found an "anarchist" garden, whose haphazard layout reflected the fact that there were no rules, and a "benevolent dictator" garden that appeared to be the garden of a single individual, with no clear boundaries between plots. It was governed by a dictator who made the rules, chose the members, laid out their plots, and selected the plants.

By 1988, Aspen Farms was a well-established garden, but it lacked a meeting place to accommodate pot-luck suppers and

visiting school groups. Students in my landscape architecture studio were asked to design a new meeting place. The students—who were white or Asian and mostly middle class—began by getting to know their clients and the neighborhood; each student stayed for a weekend with one of the gardeners. I wanted my students to understand the difference between quality of life and standard of living. You can have a high standard of living and a low quality of life. You can find people in tough situations in low-income neighborhoods who have a high quality of life, and you have to recognize and respect that. They create it for themselves with their family, with their church, or with other groups.

All the students proposed a circular or square place for meeting, a cliché. One student, John Widrick, decided to revisit Aspen Farms and ask for comments on his design for a circular meeting place in a central location. He was unprepared for the reaction of polite horror. What we had idealized as one big community was actually several smaller groups, each with its own territory and leaders. John's original scheme not only displaced several garden plots, it disposed of most of one group's territory. He began again. His new design created a meeting place by widening the central path, so the space given up to create the common area would be evenly shared. When the students presented their designs to the gardeners, they chose to build John's. The path became the garden's "main street," lined with benches and raised flower beds, which formed boundaries between the public space and adjacent garden plots. Small openings between planters were gateways leading to the garden plots beyond. Groups of plots formed small neighborhoods within the larger garden, which competed with each other for the best flower beds along the main path outside the gate to their plots. The design for Aspen Farms' main street turned conflict and competition into common benefit and has served the garden ever since.

On the ground, working with community gardeners, I learned how diverse the Mill Creek neighborhood was in terms of residents' income, employment, family history, family composition, and educational attainment. Aspen Farms took up a half block on the corner of 49th and Aspen streets. Well-kept rowhomes framed the garden on two sides; public housing faced it across 49th Street. One block down the street to the north was a vacant block. One block to the west, a third of the houses were vacant. This pattern repeated throughout the neighborhood: blocks of well-kept homes adjacent to blocks of vacant land and vacant houses.

Our maps of the neighborhood's demographics, based on 1980 US Census tracts, did not reflect what I observed on the ground. Each census tract encompassed more than thirty blocks, whose size obscured the block-to-block diversity. Data for the census tract to which Aspen Farms belonged, for example, indicated that the population included 4,227 black residents, 166 whites, 10 American Indians, and seven Filipinos. The median household income was $9,550 and the per capita income, $3,846, with 45% of the population near or below the poverty level. Nine percent of the housing units were vacant. Given the stark variation from block to block, many residents actually were much better off (with higher incomes, living on blocks with no vacancies) than the tract statistics would have predicted, and many were much worse off than the numbers indicated. Certain census data was available at the scale of the block, which clarified some factors, like the fact that although there were 166 white residents, 120 of them lived in a mental hospital. But even at the block scale the census statistics were misleading. The US Census defined a block as being bounded by streets, as opposed to a social block, with houses facing each other across a shared street. At times, the census block combined social blocks that were worlds apart. And the census had nothing to say about residents' educational attainment;

years later, I learned that people with graduate degrees may live in the same block as others who have no high school diploma, all part of the block community. Relying on statistics without field experience can take you down the wrong road. You may think you understand because you've got statistical data and you can do all sorts of calculations. But the numbers may bear little relation to reality.

The community gardeners had an intuitive understanding of natural processes in cities. Aspen Farms sloped down toward the valley bottom where Mill Creek once flowed, where it had been buried in a vast sewer. Hayward Ford knew that the soil was wetter on the garden's low end; the plots there didn't require as much irrigation as those upslope. We discussed the continuing subsidence along the buried flood plain of Mill Creek and the idea of detaining or retaining rainwater to reduce combined sewer overflows. This made sense to him, but, evidently, not to the city's planners.

After the City's 1994 Plan for West Philadelphia ignored the hazards posed by Mill Creek's buried flood plain and discounted my proposals, I decided to focus on the Mill Creek community, to inform residents about the buried floodplain, and to work together on proposals. I knew many community gardeners, but they were mostly seniors. To reach the broader adult community, I decided to work with their children. The University of Pennsylvania's Center for Community Partnerships encouraged faculty to work in West Philadelphia public schools. I met with the director, Ira Harkavy, and volunteered to work with a school, preferably a middle school, but definitely one on or near the buried floodplain. Several schools qualified, but Sulzberger Middle School was one block from Aspen Farms, and Mill Creek once flowed right through the school site. Unfortunately, the principal was resistant to having a Penn professor and students come into her school. It wasn't

until she learned about my work with Aspen Farms that she agreed to meet. Hayward Ford came with me, and so began our partnership with the garden and the school.

What began as a community-based, environmental education program organized around the urban watershed grew into a program on landscape literacy and community development, where children learned to create websites as a storytelling medium. From 1996–2001, hundreds of children at Sulzberger and students at the University of Pennsylvania learned to read the neighborhood's landscape; they traced its past, deciphered its stories, and told their own stories about its future, some of which were built. The tools they used were their own eyes and imaginations, the place itself, and historical documents such as maps, photographs, newspaper articles, census tables, and redevelopment plans. The program had four parts: reading landscape, proposing landscape change, building landscape improvements, and documenting proposals and accomplishments. The first two parts were incorporated into both university and middle-school curricula during the academic year; all four were integrated in a four-week summer program. The summer program for Sulzberger students was organized and led by my research assistants. In the mornings the group met either at Aspen Farms, where they built a pond and compost bin, or at Sulzberger, where they constructed a topographic model of the Mill Creek watershed and learned how to program a website. Their website, "SMS News," was posted on the West Philadelphia Landscape Project website.[1]

Our Mill Creek Project at Sulzberger got a lot of attention. People from foundations, from all over the country, observed the classroom. Pennsylvania's governor invited the middle school students to present their website as part of his 1998 Budget Speech to the State Legislature, which gave them a long, standing ovation. In 1999 Sulzberger was the subject of

a report on NBC Evening News. In 2000, President Bill Clinton visited the school.

Once I started working in the school I had a different relationship to adults. For example, when Hayward Ford would introduce me to someone in the neighborhood, "This is Anne Spirn, she's working with children at Sulzberger Middle School," that person would say, "Thank you. Thank you." And then they would refer to "our children," even if they didn't have any children. Where I grew up, in a predominantly white, middle-class suburb, someone would talk about "my children" or "our kids," meaning those two kids. To speak of "our children," meaning all the children of the community, was something I had never heard before. I later learned that this is common in African American communities. To take collective responsibility for all the children of a community is a tremendous asset.

The Mill Creek Coalition, a group of community leaders dedicated to improving the neighborhood, heard about my work with the school and asked me to make a presentation about the buried flood plain, where it was and what to do about it. Frances Walker, chair of the coalition's environment committee asked me to join, and, in 1999, we decided to do a pilot study to assess damage in houses on Mill Creek's buried floodplain. I proposed an area for our research and Crystal Cornitcher, president of the Mill Creek Coalition, said, "We have to include my block." "But it's not on the buried flood plain" I replied. "Yes, it is," she said, "We have terrible water problems." Crystal's block was well above the valley bottom, but the water damage was severe. Some houses had slanting floors and rotted out floorboards, some had mold on basement walls and mortar coming out of the joints between bricks in the foundation. Outside, yards sloped toward the houses, and downspouts were disconnected so that rainwater flowed into the foundations. Our pilot study led to the realization that the water issue was much bigger than

the buried floodplain, and that it likely affected a large segment of the population. This opened up an opportunity both to deal with water problems and build a local economy. Repairing roof and downspouts could be the foundation for small businesses. We would not have come to this idea without Crystal Cornitcher insisting that there was a water problem on her block. As an outsider, I would not have been able to get into people's homes and down into their basements. There were many cases like this where I would not have made important discoveries had I not been working with people in the community. We were engaged in a process of mutual teaching and learning. As I learned, my capacity for working with the community increased, as did my capacity as a researcher and as a planner and designer.

I had been meeting with engineers from the Philadelphia Water Department (PWD) since 1996, when staff of the US Environmental Protection Agency's regional water division, increasingly concerned about Philadelphia's combined sewer overflows (CSOs), had brought us together to discuss the potential of stormwater detention and green infrastructure to reduce CSOs. In 1999, Howard Neukrug, director of the PWD's newly formed Office of Watersheds asked me to take a group of engineers on a field trip to Mill Creek to show them sites appropriate for stormwater detention. An immediate outcome of our field trip was the PWD's decision to design and build demonstration projects that would detain stormwater and function as an outdoor classroom for Sulzberger Middle School. The PWD got a grant to fund the project and pledged to work with teachers and students at Sulzberger. They hired one of my research assistants to work on the project and, in 2001, co-sponsored the summer program on the urban watershed with Sulzberger and met with members of the Mill Creek Coalition.

About that time I asked an old anthropologist, "How do you know when a project is over?" "It will come to a natural

end," he said. In 2000, I had moved to Boston and the Massachusetts Institute of Technology, but continued to work with teachers at Sulzberger until 2002, when the state took over the Philadelphia School District. The state turned over the management of Sulzberger to Edison, Inc. Edison dismantled the Mill Creek Project, and key teachers left in protest. In 2009, Hayward Ford died. Two years later, Crystal Cornitcher died, and I began to understand what that anthropologist had told me. But then Fatima Williams contacted me. The last time I'd seen her, she had just graduated from Sulzberger. In 2012, I met with Fatima for the first time since 1998. She was 28 and married with three kids. She told me how learning HTML as an eighth-grader, as part of our Mill Creek Project, had led her from homelessness to a career in Web development, and I realized that I'd started out on a whole new phase of the West Philadelphia Landscape Project. I reached out to others who had been part of WPLP at some point during three decades: teachers and children (now adults, like Fatima) from Sulzberger, community leaders, professional colleagues, former research assistants. What they told me was revelatory. The teachers described how the project had transformed their careers and the entire school. Howard Neukrug, newly appointed as Philadelphia Water Commissioner, recalled how our field trip to Mill Creek led to Philadelphia's acclaimed plan: Green City, Clean Waters.[2]

With the US Environmental Protection Agency threatening to levy huge fines on the city for polluting water, Neukrug had persuaded the PWD to reduce combined sewer overflows through green infrastructure. Their plan, Green City, Clean Waters—now recognized as a landmark of policy, planning, and engineering—calls for reducing impervious surfaces in the city by 30% by 2020 in order to capture the first inch of rain to fall in a storm. If the plan works, it will save the city billions of dollars and provide the benefits of jobs, educational opportunities, and neighborhood development. But will it work (physically), and can it be done (economically, politically)?

To help test and refine Philadelphia's plan, in 2010 and 2011, my MIT students studied the ultra-urban Mill Creek Watershed. During their fieldwork, they encountered many questions from residents who were curious about what they were doing. When the students described the Green City, Clean Waters program, people were skeptical. "No jobs, no hope," one man told them. His response inspired them to propose a program that connects low-income communities with "green-collar" jobs through education, job-training, and the construction of local prototypes. My Ecological Urbanism class at MIT continues to study the Mill Creek watershed and to make proposals that integrate environmental restoration, community development, and the empowerment of youth, taking a top-down/bottom-up approach that brings together public officials and neighborhood residents. In 2015 I co-taught the class with Mami Hara, then chief of staff at the PWD. Our students devised Philadelphia Green Schools, integrating three movements—green schoolyards, community schools, and place-based education— where schools are at the heart of community development.

In 2018, my work in West Philadelphia took a new turn. Frances Walker called for help. After her mother died, her dream was to move back to the family home, but she was in poor health, on a tiny fixed income, and the house was uninhabitable. Rain poured in through a hole in the roof, mold had taken hold, and Frances didn't have the $15,000 for repairs. Philadelphia has a program to help low-income homeowners maintain their homes, but Frances didn't qualify because she did not have clear title to the house. Nor did anyone else. Her mother died without a will. There were 17 heirs, including Frances. The home was an "heir house" with a "tangled" deed. Frances knew what happens to such houses. Without a title, family members

cannot sell the house, and clearing the title is a prolonged and costly process. The heirs can't agree what to do, and the houses sit and deteriorate. Then they are torn down.

In neighborhoods across Philadelphia (and the US), thousands of houses stand vacant because no one has clear title to the property. The abandonment of a single rowhouse exposes adjacent properties to risk from rot, mold, vermin, fire, and the potential for illegal activities carried on by squatters in the abandoned property. Waiting to address these problems after houses are abandoned and after they deteriorate and collapse is expensive. Widespread abandonment depletes the city's housing stock and creates another problem: extensive, scattered vacant land.

Meanwhile, after more than a half century of redlining and disinvestment, outside capital is flowing into West Philadelphia's low-income, African-American neighborhoods, and homeowners are losing their homes through predatory lending (reverse-redlining) and the unscrupulous practices of aggressive speculators. To make matters worse, tangled deeds make it difficult for heirs to claim a deceased relative's property. These neighborhoods are in dire need of investment, but not through tricking and cheating residents out of their homes. My students and I are working with Monumental Baptist Church and its community development corporation, to develop an action plan to address this crisis and to study how flows of capital, like flows of water, shape the landscape of West Philadelphia.

There are tremendous advantages to staying engaged in a single place over many years. You build trust with people, you build relationships, not just with people who live in the place, but also with those who are working for public agencies or in the community as teachers. Over time, you accumulate knowledge, build networks, and gain understanding that those who work in a place for only a few years can never know. When you are in a place over time, making a series of proposals, staying engaged, watching what happens, evaluating the results, was it a success, was it a failure, adapting, you learn a tremendous amount.

To test my ideas, I put them on the line in the form of actions. When there's a failure, it reveals a flaw in the theory: it didn't encompass enough or it didn't take certain things into account, things that had been invisible to me until the failure revealed them. I may start out with one idea, and then, the process of action and reflection modifies that idea or generates a new one. Some of the most important ideas that I developed over the course of these last 30 years emerged from the work, they were not ideas that I already had when I started. For example, in Boston, when I found a correlation between large swaths of vacant land and the buried floodplains of former streams, that discovery emerged from looking for ways to restore the urban natural environment and trying to explain the patterns of vacant land I found in low-income neighborhoods. At first, I didn't regard water as key, that realization emerged from the research, when I made the connection between vacant valley bottoms, buried sewers, and polluted harbor. Then the failure to convince city planners and engineers to consider my proposals revealed barriers to innovation in urban design and planning that would need to be overcome. In action research, one thing leads to another.

My research has been enhanced and enlarged and in some cases transformed by my relationships and experiences in this community. When I started out I didn't think of youth as probably the most important agents for change in a neighborhood like Mill Creek; I went into the middle school in order to reach the adults. What I discovered once I started working in the middle school was how fresh and open, imaginative, intelligent, and

ready to act these young people were. So I expanded my research questions. How can urban design and planning restore the urban natural environment, rebuild neighborhoods, and empower youth, simultaneously and synergistically? How can this be accomplished in ways that are just, so that people who live in a place are not displaced? How can designers and planners weave together threads of environment, poverty, race, social equity, and educational reform, along with aesthetics and function? For the past 35 years I have sought to demonstrate how this might be accomplished and to develop theory and methods to support this kind of practice. The partnership with people of the Mill Creek community, engaging with them in a mutual process of teaching and learning, has been fundamental and indispensable, a source of insight, inspiration, and friendship.

1 *West Philadelphia Landscape Project*, https://wplp.net/index.html#.

2 See "Stories," *West Philadelphia Landscape Project*, https://wplp.net/stories/.

Above and previous: A collection of moments from the West Philadelphia Landscape Project 1987–2018. Collages by Melissa Isador.

FRANCESCA RUSSELLO AMMON

GREEN GLUE
URBAN RENEWAL IN POSTWAR PHILADELPHIA

Francesca Russello Ammon is an associate professor of City & Regional Planning and Historic Preservation at the University of Pennsylvania Stuart Weitzman School of Design. A social and cultural historian of the built environment, Ammon is the author of *Bulldozer: Demolition and Clearance of the Postwar Landscape* [Yale University Press, 2016]. She is currently writing a history of postwar preservation and urban renewal based upon the case study of Society Hill in Philadelphia.

HISTORY, PLANNING, URBAN DESIGN

By 1965, nearly 800 American cities—located in almost every state across the country—sought to spur revitalization through the federal policy of urban renewal. Typically, their efforts took the form of large-scale demolition aimed at clearing space for new, modern construction.[1] Simultaneously, cities remade their aging downtowns in service to the automobile, welcoming new highways in place of formerly dense urban development. As these projects tore down buildings, they also ripped apart existing communities. Over the course of the entire urban renewal program, from the Housing Act of 1949 through 1980, the policy displaced nearly a million families and over a hundred thousand businesses.[2]

While Philadelphia implemented its own share of clearance-based renewal projects, the city often applied a more targeted approach that joined demolition with rehabilitation and small-scale infill development. *Architectural Forum* termed this the Philadelphia Cure – "clearing cities with penicillin, not surgery."[3] Philadelphia also distinguished itself by attempting to balance the competing demands of automobile growth with pedestrian-oriented designs. This article uses the case of Society Hill, Philadelphia's landmark preservation-based urban renewal project, to show how attempts to knit together a cohesive new community simultaneously required the destruction of an existing one.[4]

Society Hill, a roughly four-block by seven-block, 116-acre area in eastern Center City, is one of Philadelphia's oldest neighborhoods. Known as Washington Square East in official postwar planning documents, the area was christened Society Hill as part of its urban renewal rebranding. The name came from the Free Society of Traders, a joint-stock company of English Quakers who settled along the Delaware River following William Penn's arrival in 1682. As Society Hill developed, its dense row houses along major thoroughfares became home to the city's wealthy elites, while tradespeople and servants lived on the narrower back alleys and courts. By 1950, the area's socioeconomic character had changed dramatically. Concentrated on the neighborhood's southern edge, African Americans made up nearly 20% of the population of Society Hill. Eastern European Jews, especially Russians, Poles, and Austrians, encompassed an even more substantial contingent. Median income across the neighborhood was just over half the city average. Rents and real estate values were also below average, and only one-fifth of the dwelling units were owner-occupied.[5]

Opposite: Illustration of part of Edmund Bacon's greenway plan for Society Hill, Philadelphia.

1 Francesca Russello Ammon, *Bulldozer: Demolition and Clearance of the Postwar Landscape* (Yale University Press, 2016), 144.

2 Herbert J. Gans, *The Urban Villagers: Group and Class in the Life of Italian-Americans* (Free Press, 1982), 384–85.

3 "The Philadelphia Cure: Clearing Slums with Penicillin, Not Surgery," *Architectural Forum* (1952), 112–19.

4 For more on the preservation-based approach to the urban renewal of Society Hill, see Francesca Russello Ammon, "Picture Preservation: Picturing Preservation: Photographs as Urban Renewal Planning Knowledge in Society Hill, Philadelphia," *Journal of Planning Education and Research* (December 5, 2018), https://doi.org/10.1177/0739456X18815742.

5 US Bureau of the Census, *US Census of Population: 1950* (US Government Printing Office, 1952), Tract 5-A.

6 Gregory Donofrio, "Attacking Distribution: Obsolescence and Efficiency of Food Markets in the Age of Urban Renewal," *Journal of Planning History* 13, no. 2 (May 2014): 136–59, https://doi.org/10.1177/1538513213507540.

7 Edmund Bacon, "Address to the Annual Meeting of the City Parks Association, Subject: Rehabilitation of Old Philadelphia (Society Hill)," June 14, 1950, 4, Box 292.III.A.4, Edmund N. Bacon Collection 292, Architectural Archives, University of Pennsylvania.

8 Wright, Andrade & Amenta Architects, *Washington Square East Urban Renewal Area: Technical Report* (Philadelphia Redevelopment Authority, May 1959).

9 Peter Binzen, "He Planted the Seeds: Now, Center City is a Greener Place," *Philadelphia Inquirer* (October 24, 1994), G3.

10 Wright, Andrade & Amenta Architects, Washington Square East Urban Renewal Area, 40.

11 Edmund Bacon, "Urban Development I: Urban Redevelopment – An Opportunity for City Rebuilding," in *Planning, 1949: Proceedings of the Annual Planning Conference held in Cleveland, Ohio, 10–12 October 1949* (ASPO, 1950).

12 Ibid, 23.

13 J. Hardin Peterson, in US Congress, House of Representatives, Committee on the Public Lands, *Philadelphia National Park Commission*, 78th Congress, 1st session (April 11, 1945), 59–60.

14 Madeline L. Cohen, "Postwar City Planning in Philadelphia: Edmund N. Bacon and the Design of Washington Square East" (PhD diss., University of Pennsylvania, 1991), 427–28.

15 Edmund N. Bacon, "A Case Study in Urban Design," *Journal of the American Institute of Planners* 26, no. 3 (August 1960): 225–26.

In 1959, planners designated the neighborhood for urban renewal, hoping to attract a higher-income demographic to update its physical character and increase the city's tax base. By targeting the restoration of single-family homes in a largely residential area, they aimed to offer a modern, yet historically rich alternative to the growing suburbs. In Unit 1, 65 acres located in the northeastern part of the area, the city replaced an outdated, largely immigrant-operated wholesale food market with three 32-story high-rise towers designed by I.M. Pei.[6] Architects Pei and Louis Sauer also built substantial developments of new townhouses in the towers' vicinity. In the 50-acre southern portion of the neighborhood, Unit 2, the Redevelopment Authority relied more strongly upon the rehabilitation of existing row houses. According to the city's planning commissioner, Edmund Bacon, this rehabilitation would primarily be accomplished by "restoring cornices, cleaning bricks, painting and replacing structures."[7] Even more substantially, the Redevelopment Authority marked industrial properties for acquisition and removal, required the conversion of mixed-use and multi-family properties to single-family residential, and designated for demolition a range of properties needed for the expansion of schools, hospitals, and religious institutions.[8]

Designers also introduced a network of pedestrian greenways that would cohere the historic area and connect it with the also-transforming area surrounding Independence Hall to the north. According to Bacon, these wide brick pathways sprinkled with tree plantings and occasional benches were to be "the glue that holds Society Hill together."[9] Planning documents predicted that this "working and visual armature for the neighborhood" would provide new means of integration and access, public spaces for socializing, and pathways for opening urban design sightlines between existing community institutions.[10]

Bacon viewed these community institutions–many of them religious–as a foundation for providing the area with "new dignity and significance through site planning."[11] He recalled an occasion of "walking through a fairly dull two-story brick row house section of Philadelphia," but then coming upon and entering a Baroque church. "It was a rich contrast to be suddenly plunged into its shadowy interior with its rising spacious vaults," he observed. "After leaving the church I saw the old street with new eyes. The daily experience of everyone who lives there, the attitude toward the area, must be influenced by the knowledge of what the building has to offer. The character of the church infuses the entire area with a different kind of feeling than it otherwise would have."[12] The transformative visual potential of key landmarks, like this church, would significantly shape Bacon's approach to Society Hill.

The idea for the greenways originated during the creation of Independence National Historic Park. In 1945, Congress held hearings to consider the creation of a federal park in and around Independence Hall, where America's Constitution and Declaration of Independence were debated and signed. As

J. Hardin Peterson, chairman of the Committee on the Public Lands, noted during the hearings, several important civic institutions were located near each other. But landmarks like Carpenters' Hall (where the first Continental Congress met in 1774) and the Second Bank of the United States had become lost amidst the density that had grown up around them. "When you come in there now, you drive up and you are on top of the thing before you realize it," he lamented. "The idea is to clear out the old buildings in between and [create] one memorial group... with parkways."[13] Architect Roy Larson conceived of a system of pathways that would cut through the interior blocks near Independence Hall, leaving existing 19th-century commercial structures on the edges, but clearing away interior buildings to open up sightlines between historic colonial structures.[14]

Bacon built upon this idea for pedestrian connectors in the model of Philadelphia that he included in the Better Philadelphia Exhibition of 1947. More than 400,000 Philadelphians visited this major public expo, held at Gimbel's department store, to see the vision for their city's future.[15] Relative to Larson's axial proposal, Bacon designed more sensitive and intimate, less formal "historic pathways." He further proposed extending these pathways south, into Society Hill, to connect the historic neighborhood with the historic park.[16] When the city and individual developers introduced specific redevelopment plans for the neighborhood, they made these greenways a key element.[17]

The greenways provoked criticism in Society Hill, however, as they required the destruction of existing buildings to make way for their development. In some locations, planners sited greenways for existing mid-block streets that they would just permanently close. This occurred along the stretch of St. Peter's Way (now called St. Joseph's Way) located to the north of Spruce Street. Although this greenway section followed the former route of Orianna Street, its full realization still required the removal of all but one row of four buildings fronting on the street.[18] But existing roadways did not sufficiently fulfill the planners' needs. With many inner blocks already fully built up, only demolition would clear the way to insert entirely new pathways.

Charles Peterson, an architect and historian with the National Parks Service who had moved to Society Hill in 1951, was the loudest critic of the greenways plan. Considered by many to be an architectural purist, Peterson pushed back against the Redevelopment Authority's demolition plans when they affected a number of the neighborhood's then 550 historically certified buildings. The Philadelphia Historical Commission had surveyed the neighborhood at the start of urban renewal, aiming to identify the most prized properties from a historical perspective and hoping that redevelopers would restore, rather than destroy, these properties wherever possible. The Historical Commission's criteria for certification included the building's having "been identified by documented fact or by long-established legend with important or interesting events or people," or having "stood so long as to be a valuable example of architectural design and construction."[19] Despite these

16 Ibid., 429.

17 The low-income African American neighborhood of Mill Creek, located five miles west of Society Hill, was also among Philadelphia's first urban renewal projects. There, architect Louis Kahn was incorporating greenways into a plan for public housing. Bacon told a reporter, "What is really exciting is that we are expanding this greenway concept into other parts of the city. It isn't just for the historic Society Hill section." George H. Favre, "Multi-use Greenways to Adorn Philadelphia Renewal Areas," *Christian Science Monitor* (November 29, 1968), 7. On Bacon's urban renewal plans for neighborhoods throughout Philadelphia, see Gregory Heller, *Ed Bacon: Planning, Politics, and the Building of Modern Philadelphia* (University of Pennsylvania Press, 2013).

18 Wright, Andrade & Amenta Architects, *Washington Square East Urban Renewal Area*, 43.

19 "Minutes of the Advisory Commission on Historic Buildings Meeting," April 9, 1957, Box A-679, Folder: PHC, 1957, Historical Commission Files, City Archives of Philadelphia.

20 William J. Eiman to Barbara Snow (August 6, 1962), Box A-10485, Folder: OPDC (1 of 2), Historical Commission Files, City Archives of Philadelphia.

21 "Minutes of the Philadelphia Historical Commission Meeting," February 24, 1959, Box A-679, Folder: PHC, 1958, Historical Commission Files, City Archives of Philadelphia.

22 1940 is the date of the most recently released long-form census data; US Bureau of the Census, *1940 United States Federal Census*, Ancestry.com (accessed January 6, 2020).

23 Carole Abercauph, interview transcript (November 5, 2008), *Project Philadelphia 19106*, Special Collections Research Center, Temple University Libraries, also available at Preserving Society Hill, http://pennds.org/societyhill/.

24 US Renewal Assistance Administration. *Urban Renewal Project Characteristics* (US GPO, June 30, 1966). On attempts to rehouse some of the displaced within Society Hill, see Francesca Russello Ammon, "Resisting Gentrification Amid Historic Preservation: Society Hill, Philadelphia and the Fight for Low-Income Housing," *Change Over Time* 8, no. 1 (2018): 8–31, https://muse.jhu.edu/article/717926.

25 Jane Jacobs, *The Death and Life of Great American Cities* (Vintage Books, 1992), 416.

26 Elizabeth Browne, interview transcript (October 13, 2009), *Project Philadelphia 19106*. This being a city, the secluded greenways were also occasionally the sites of street crime like muggings: Jean Pomeroy,

designations, the original Society Hill urban renewal plans marked approximately 100 historically certified buildings for demolition.[20] Peterson worked both to reduce this number and to add more buildings to the certified list.

One of Peterson's major arguments with Bacon occurred during the siting of the southern portion of St. Peter's Way. The city planned to tear down some vacant city buildings, including an old police facility, to create a passive recreational park and playground now known as Delancey Park, or Three Bears Park. Bacon proposed to run a greenway through the park in a line that would connect St. Joseph's Church, to the north, with St. Peter's Church, to the south. Peterson did not dispute the park plan as it did not directly affect any historic properties or existing residences; his concern was with the stretch of buildings between Pine and Delancey Streets, particularly 312 and 314 Delancey Street, two historically certified buildings that stood in the way of the greenway.

The Historical Commission defended the two buildings. The owner-occupant of number 312 was willing to restore the building to the Redevelopment Authority's standards if they would agree not to demolish it. In early 1959, the Chairman of the Commission, Grant Simon, and G. Holmes Perkins, dean of the University of Pennsylvania's Graduate School of Fine Arts and head of the Design Advisory Board that oversaw new construction, discussed the sites. Simon told Perkins, "In the opinion of the Commission, the buildings are more important than the greenway." He was working with one of the consultants who had developed the plan in order to identify an alternative location for it. One proposal was to move the greenway slightly west, to the site of 316 Delancey Street – a non-historic property that was then vacant. Yet Perkins urged completion of the original plan.[21] This would ensure alignment of the greenway with the vista of St. Peter's spire, a guiding principle of the design, as revealed in both drawings and photographs.

According to the 1940 census, the occupants of the buildings on the 300 block of Delancey Street were typical of Society Hill at midcentury. What had once been single-family residences were now often occupied by multiple households. Four families resided in each of 312 and 314 Delancey Street. The heads of households on the block frequently included immigrants– primarily from Russia, Poland, Austria, and Germany–while their children had been born in Pennsylvania. These were working-class families, with occupations including laborer, fireman, stevedore, tailor, cleaner, and carpenter.[22] Although census data have not yet been made publicly available for the time in question, it is likely that some of these residents had already moved on at the time of urban renewal some 20 years later. The closing of the Delancey Street fire station and diminishing dock work in the area would have directly affected at least two of these householders' occupations. Further, when urban renewal changes in zoning eliminated mixed use, those householders who conducted their businesses in the same building as their residence were often forced to move elsewhere. With most of the neighborhood composed of renters, urban renewal would also have driven out many others as owner-occupancy was generally a requirement for purchasing a property that the Redevelopment Authority had acquired. This is not to mention the financial resources required to afford restoration of what were generally multi-unit buildings to single-family homes. But no one could reside in a building that no longer existed – and that proved to be the fate of the row houses at 312 and 314 Delancey Street, despite the Historical Commission's best efforts to preserve them.

The uncertainty surrounding urban renewal also incited fears that indirectly displaced other area residents. For example, Carole Abercauph's family moved to 329 Pine Street in 1953. She was nine years old at the time. Her mother was from Poland, while her father, a jeweler, had been born in Philadelphia. When the Abercauphs moved in, they occupied two floors of the building as the family's apartment; their son and his family resided in another unit. Talk of the creation of St. Peter's Way worried them, however. Carole recalled of her mother, "She didn't want to move, but she was convinced that the Redevelopment Authority, which had broad powers at that time, would take our property, because it was the only one that went all the way through to Delancey Street," thus simplifying both property acquisition and clearance. To get ahead of the displacement process, the family sold their house;[23] though, this ultimately proved unnecessary since their property did not offer the important vistas so prized by the planners. Across the entire Society Hill urban renewal project, the Redevelopment Authority counted 580 families displaced by urban renewal; but families like the Abercauphs, and others who moved in anticipation of government acquisition, were not counted in such totals, suggesting a larger toll.[24]

Today, the greenways are an integral and much-appreciated asset of the neighborhood. Despite Jane Jacobs's criticism that "the planning commission's pet esthetic creations, the Greenway 'promenades,' do not have the physical appearance in reality that they had in the planners' renderings," landscape architect John Collins's sketches for these elements were largely realized in Society Hill.[25] Photographs from the 1960s show the walks in immediate use by residents, just as he had anticipated. Windows built into former party walls hide the scars of demolition, making it difficult to discern that there was ever a time when these walkways did not exist. When asked how it was to raise a young family in Society Hill, one urban renewal arrival replied, "Well, it was a lot more fun, I think, because we were out walking around all the time with the baby carriage and the stroller and whatnot. It was more of a challenge than other places, but it was great... Delancey Park or Three Bears Park opened up about that time, so that was a great magnet for us all, and much of the social life was there."[26] Another resident redeveloper put his assessment of the greenway system more succinctly: "To me, it's the best thing in Society Hill."[27]

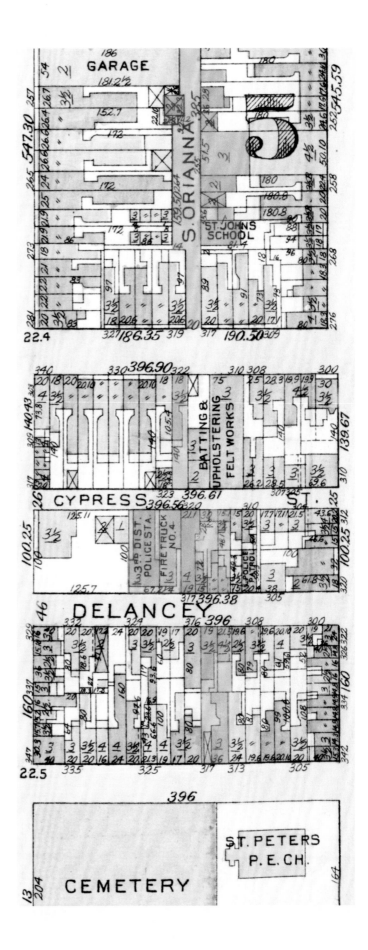

Right: Orange indicates properties cleared or repurposed related to the Society Hill greenway plan.

Although an early proposal anticipated connecting Washington Square (in Society Hill) with Rittenhouse Square (on the western side of Center City) as a means to energize the full city, these broader greenway extensions never materialized.[28] But the original design did expand to both Franklin Square to the north and the waterfront to the east. Bacon's discussion of them in his widely-read *Design of Cities* also helped spread greenways beyond Philadelphia.[29] Closer to home, the greenways connected the redeveloped neighborhood internally, leading residents playfully from park to community institutions; and they also offered inroads from outside the immediate area, inviting others in to explore.

These gains, however, came at a cost. In both representation and practice, urban renewal offered new openings to create a new community. But, in the process, these openings erased many of the homes, livelihoods, and lived landscapes of another community. By 1980, Society Hill's population was down to 5,200 (versus nearly 7,000 in 1950). Median income was 2.5 times the city average (versus half the city average before), and 64% of adults had completed college (versus only 4% before renewal). Owner occupancy had doubled, with the new Society Hill Towers accounting for many of the renters.[30] To be sure, the greenways were only one small piece of this larger process. But they illustrate the ways in which attempts to attract one new population led planners and landscape architects to tread heavily on another. If the greenways acted as a glue—as Bacon once claimed—it was a glue that was particularly necessary in order to cohere a social and material environment that some of the city's own actions had torn asunder.

interview transcript (January 15, 2010), *Project Philadelphia 19106*.

27 Hugh Scott, "The Society Hill of Tomorrow," *Philadelphia Inquirer Magazine* (January 12, 1958), 12–13; Robert Parsky, interview transcript (May 5, 2008), *Project Philadelphia 19106*.

28 Damon Childs, interview transcript (November 18, 1992), Edmund N. Bacon Research Collection, 1973–2004, Architectural Archives, University of Pennsylvania; Scott, ibid.

29 Edmund N. Bacon, *Design of Cities* (Viking, 1967).

30 US Bureau of the Census, *US Census of Population and Housing: 1980* (US Government Printing Office, 1983), Tract 10; US Bureau of the Census, US Census of Housing: 1950 (US Government Printing Office, 1953), Tract 5-A.

IN CONVERSATION WITH
JESSICA HENSON

What began as a pro-bono research initiative undertaken by Gehry Partners, OLIN, and Geosyntec in 2014 became, in 2016, the *LA River Index* – a web-based visualization that brings together data from all 51 miles of the urban river into a consistent and accessible format. Today, the design team has a variety of active projects along the Los Angeles River, including the LA River Master Plan. Jessica Henson, of OLIN's Los Angeles office, has been involved in the effort from the start. Her work on the LA River dovetails with her academic research on freshwater landscapes and the recently published *Fresh Water: Design Research for Inland Water Territories*, which focuses on the shared hydrosocial histories and water issues of the major inland watersheds of North America. **Rebecca Popowsky** spoke to Henson about the LA River and the challenges of engaging communities in large-scale design projects.

+ The LA River Master Plan encompasses 51 miles of the Los Angeles River and 17 cities. Can you briefly describe the river and its community context?

The Los Angeles River flows for 51 miles from the neighborhood of Canoga Park in the west San Fernando Valley to the City of Long Beach where it meets the Pacific Ocean. On this journey it flows parallel to the Santa Monica Mountains, around Griffith Park, through Downtown LA, past some of the heaviest industry in LA County, and through the southeast LA cities, such as Cudahy, Bell Gardens, South Gate, and Compton, before reaching the river mouth. In total it passes 17 river-adjacent municipalities including the areas of LA County with the highest levels of environmental pollution.

Before intensive settlement, the flash-flood prone LA River often flooded due to the characteristics of the steep watershed. Oftentimes the river would be entirely dry in the San Fernando Valley and south of Downtown LA, and would then quickly swell to overflowing after a large storm. As the LA region grew and development intensified, homes and industry were built right up to the edge of the riverbed and the river became a threat to life and property. Efforts to channelize the river began in the late 1800s and were completed after a series of devastating floods in the 1930s. Now, the LA River is entirely fenced and channelized, and most of it is lined with concrete.

As a result, the river system today is largely separated from our social and ecological communities. For the better part of the 20th century, the LA River was treated merely as drainage infrastructure with the singular job of getting water to the Pacific Ocean as fast as possible. Given this role, most communities along the banks of the river turned their backs to the river, and it became a place associated with illicit activities, industry, and pollution. Most people today would recognize the channelized, concrete form of the LA River as the setting for a number of epic Hollywood movie car chases.

The potential uses of the river, beyond simple flood conveyance, have only really started to be explored in the last couple of decades. Remarkably, the LA River right-of-way includes over 2,300 acres of publicly owned land, and since the river runs through some of the most underserved communities in southeast LA and the west San Fernando Valley, the potential of the river to move the needle as a multi-benefit community resource is significant. Along the Lower River, parkland in some communities is as low as 0.8 acres per thousand people, vastly below the LA County goal of four acres per thousand people and even below the World Health Organization recommendation of 2.25 acres. In Los Angeles County, where land prices are soaring and park needs are high, 2,300 acres of publicly accessible open space could make a big difference if community needs can be balanced with flood realities and safety.

+ Designing at this scale is a monumental task in any context. How has the design team managed this complexity and what issues have emerged as most central?

There are many layers to the complexity of the LA River. First, the jurisdictional complexity can make decision making complicated. The LA County Flood Control District and the US Army Corps of Engineers each operate and maintain roughly half of the river. The river crosses through all five LA County supervisorial districts, 17 river-adjacent cities, 23 City of LA neighborhoods, and four LA County unincorporated areas, so the challenge is to bring these varied constituencies into the conversation and understand what their unique decision drivers are. For some groups, such as the Army Corps, they have a core mission, while for others they are serving a specific constituency.

When our team started studying the LA River, one of the first steps we took was to create a river mile system. Since the LA River was never used significantly for navigation, it didn't have a river mile numbering system like many rivers in the US. Each of the entities that work along the river have historically had their own numbering and reach designations, which can lead to confusion when you are trying to identify a specific location on the river. While a 51-mile numbering system might not seem significant, it had a huge effect on our inventory and analysis and community engagement process because it was possible to bring data from various sources into a singular reference system. Also, the 51-mile number system with Long Beach at mile zero and Canoga Park at mile 51 helps communities along the LA River to understand that they are part of a larger system and river community.

The river mile system and our research from 2014–2016 was brought together on the *LA River Index* in 2016, a grant-funded website focused on compiling the team's research in a format that would allow users to engage with the river through topics of interest to them, ranging from flood risk, water supply, and water quality to parks, ecology, equity, public health, transportation, and programming. The website was designed to bring data together for all 51 miles, recognizing the complexity of jurisdictions and communities along the river's banks.

Beginning in 2018, the team began the LA River Master Plan with LA County. The research and knowledge gathered for the *LA River Index* was a starting point in terms of data, but the master plan process has taken it much further. Through the analysis process and community engagement, we identified nine goals for the master plan and focused detailed inventory and analysis in each of these areas: flood risk reduction, parks, ecosystems, access, arts and culture, education and engagement, housing affordability, water supply, and water quality.

+ Did those nine goals come into focus as you learned more about the river and its context?

Yes, absolutely. When we started we knew we needed to understand the flood risk aspects of the LA River channel and the relationship of the watershed hydrology and channel hydraulics. As we started digging deeper into the data, it became evident that the LA River flows through some of the most underserved communities of LA County, especially along the lower river where park need in terms of total acreage and access is significantly higher than the upper river. Additionally, environmental pollution along most of the lower river is in the worst 5–10% of living conditions in the state of California. Many of the lower river communities are predominantly Hispanic, and some are largely immigrant communities where Spanish is often a primary language spoken in households. The average age is lower than the LA County average, meaning there are many young people who are experiencing poor environmental living conditions adjacent to industry and poor air quality due to the 710 Freeway, which parallels the lower river. As we filled out our research, it became clear that housing affordability is becoming even more challenging in these areas, and many of the communities don't have policies in place to protect tenants. As we layered information together, environmental pollution, chronic health issues, and housing affordability became key factors driving our research.

As a result, topics related to affordable housing and persons experiencing homelessness have come to the forefront of our work. Many people use the LA River channel as their home, setting up encampments and tents under bridges or in areas of dense vegetation. The issues along the LA River related to homelessness are some of the most layered and complex in the country. Encampments are causing significant water quality and sanitation issues for maintenance crews and community members at outreach meetings often cite persons experiencing homelessness as the reason they don't visit the river. Meanwhile, the number of people experiencing homelessness in LA County continues to rise and is now over 60,000. As we've continued to study the river, coming up with solutions for interim housing and sanitation stations has become a core part of our research and design goals.

+ When dealing with topics that are so wide ranging, I imagine that methodology is always a central question, both in terms of gathering information and in terms of visualizing that information. What are some primary methods of analysis and representation that have proven useful?

In 2015 and 2016 when we started drawing the 51-mile river system and overlapping data sets to look for areas of high need for parks, water quality improvements, ecosystem function, water supply projects, and improved access it quickly became clear that the graphic quality would be so muddy by the time we layered datatogether that it wouldn't be legible. A few of us in the office had been testing ideas for representation of linear systems for a couple years at this point. I had used linearized representation of hydraulics, hydrology, and social data for research I was doing along the Mississippi River and my colleagues at OLIN had tested similar strategies for other projects. When we began work on the LA River Master Plan in 2018 and started to formalize our research, our team quickly started using linear referencing for data along the 51-mile LA River and worked to develop a methodology to linearize over 200 datasets.

We quickly saw the benefit of using these "LA River Rulers" (see examples on the next page) to bring water data, social data, and environment data into the same representational format regardless of which consultant on the wider team had done the research or created the data, thereby making it possible to look for patterns, typologies, and connections along the 51 miles of the river across varied subject matter areas. For the first time it became easy to compare datasets along the river, reading the rulers almost like a series of DNA strands.

From the 200 datasets we analyzed—some of which were existing and some that the team created—we were able to work with the project steering committee to determine which datasets were the most critical to understand needs along the river in relation to the nine goals of the master plan. This was an interesting process because different people have different priorities for the river and thinking about the river requires making tough choices. For instance, when thinking about habitat, do we prioritize protecting the intact habitat areas and creating buffers around them or do we focus on creating new habitat areas? Obviously, both are critically important, but since resources aren't endless, you have to start somewhere. These are the types of needs we were evaluating. Ultimately, we landed on a system of evaluation that could weight various datasets differently. For example, existing habitat could be weighted at 50%, buffer areas at 20%, possible linkages at 15%, and areas in need of habitat at 15%. This started to give some datasets more impact on the needs assessment.

+ Analyzing this river landscape has meant more than researching the physical site and its social and economic context. In order to understand the river, you had to also understand other peoples' plans for it. I understand there are 140 community, regional, and river-related plans, as well as bike and pedestrian plans, general plans, and design guidelines that have accrued over recent decades. How did you go about analyzing this complex policy and planning landscape?

Yes, since the Olmsted-Bartholomew Regional Plan of 1929, there has been no shortage of thinking and planning for the LA River. That plan was visionary in its goals for recreational and environmental connectivity across the region, but unfortunately it was never realized, likely due to a whole range of issues including the Great Depression, catastrophic flooding in the 1930s, and developer-driven decision making. Instead of the parkway imagined by the plan, manufacturing industries and critical transportation rail and highway networks filled in around the LA River and the channelization of the river, which had begun in the 1800s, was completed in the 1940s and 1950s.

The LA County 1996 Master Plan for the river was the first official planning document that began to imagine the concrete LA River as more than just a flood channel, recognizing that recreational paths, habitat corridors, and parks could be placed alongside the river to provide community connectivity and benefit. Numerous advocacy groups, such as Friends of the LA River (founded in 1985), began to inspire a generation of Angelenos to think differently about the LA River.

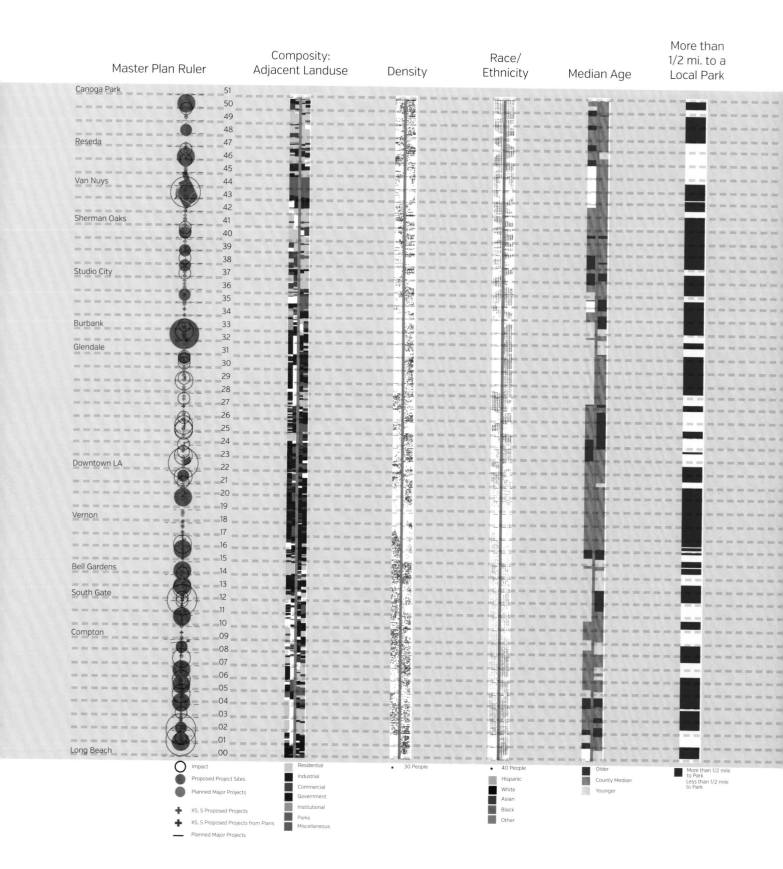

Master Plan Ruler		Composity: Adjacent Landuse	Density	Race/ Ethnicity	Median Age	More than 1/2 mi. to a Local Park

Canoga Park — 51
— 50
— 49
— 48
Reseda — 47
— 46
— 45
Van Nuys — 44
— 43
— 42
Sherman Oaks — 41
— 40
— 39
— 38
Studio City — 37
— 36
— 35
— 34
Burbank — 33
— 32
Glendale — 31
— 30
— 29
— 28
— 27
— 26
— 25
— 24
— 23
Downtown LA — 22
— 21
— 20
— 19
Vernon — 18
— 17
— 16
— 15
Bell Gardens — 14
— 13
South Gate — 12
— 11
— 10
Compton — 09
— 08
— 07
— 06
— 05
— 04
— 03
— 02
— 01
Long Beach — 00

Legend:
○ Impact
● Proposed Project Sites
● Planned Major Projects
✚ XS, S Proposed Projects
✚ XS, S Proposed Projects from Plans
— Planned Major Projects

Residential
Industrial
Commercial
Government
Institutional
Parks
Miscellaneous

• 30 People
• 40 People

Hispanic
White
Asian
Black
Other

Older
County Median
Younger

More than 1/2 mile to Park
Less than 1/2 mile to Park

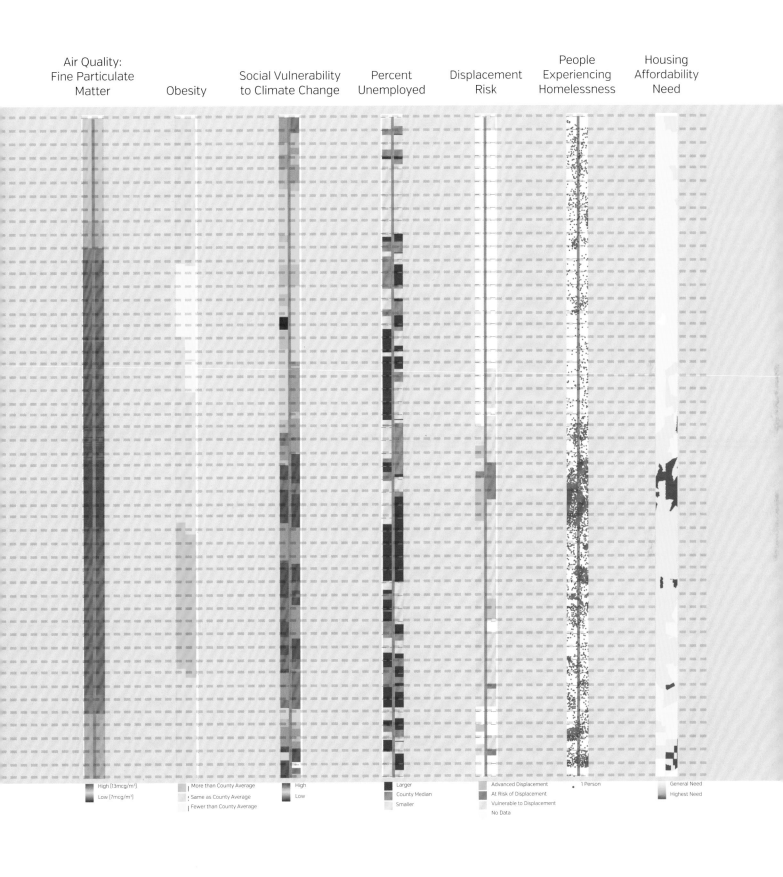

Air Quality:
Fine Particulate
Matter

Obesity

Social Vulnerability
to Climate Change

Percent
Unemployed

Displacement
Risk

People
Experiencing
Homelessness

Housing
Affordability
Need

High [13mcg/m³]
Low [7mcg/m³]

More than County Average
Same as County Average
Fewer than County Average

High
Low

Larger
County Median
Smaller

Advanced Displacement
At Risk of Displacement
Vulnerable to Displacement
No Data

1 Person

General Need
Highest Need

Since the 1996 plan, the number of planning documents that reference the potential of the LA River continues to increase as local neighborhoods and municipalities recognize the possible community and ecological benefits of connecting to the LA River. Unfortunately, though, many of the plans only cover a specific stretch of the river and they don't work together. This became a primary objective of our team. We didn't want to just layer another separate strategy onto the already complex number of plans: we wanted to read all of those plans to understand the good and the bad, the possible and the impossible, and to establish a vision for 51 miles of connected open space.

The literature review of the 140 planning documents took our team months to complete and we worked to create a database with all the known projects that were in some level of development across the watershed. In a way, this map of over 1,500 known projects across the 834-square-mile watershed became our new base map. The database includes not only very large municipal and county driven projects such as a City of LA Taylor Yard project and a new bridge in Long Beach, but also smaller neighborhood-scale green streets, curb cuts, and trails being driven by local non-profits and community members. We didn't need to plan projects where people already had good ideas, but where existing projects weren't meeting community needs along the mainstem of the river, we wanted to know. There is a need for projects at many scales within the watershed and along the river, ranging from small interventions such as shade structures and benches to large regional parks and crossings. Each project has a role to play in setting up a successful cadence along the river.

+ Any conversation about an ecological revitalization of the LA River is necessarily followed by questions about potential impacts to the communities that it runs through. How are policy-makers and designers addressing questions of equity and displacement?

In LA County living along the beach or in the mountains is expensive and these natural features are seen as amenities. When mapping housing and land value, parcels adjacent to the LA River do not show this type of indication. In fact, in some areas, you could make the argument that being adjacent to the river is a blight on the parcels. But, if the LA River becomes a 51-mile connected open space, with rich ecological function, recreation, connective trails, and arts and culture amenities, living next to the river will inevitably become appealing.

Our team has studied other linear projects, such as the 606 Trail in Chicago and the Atlanta Beltline to find housing and displacement trends where affordable housing policies were not in place before improvements began. Research shows that, due to land speculation, a significant amount of property value increase happens before projects are even completed. This means that for the LA River, we can't wait until park projects are under development to think about affordable housing. If a neighborhood has enough affordable housing, runaway market property value and rent increases that cause significant displacement can be held in check.

We've been working with Rick Jacobus—whose firm Street Level Advisors focuses on housing affordability—and housing experts across LA County ranging from county departments to non-profit organizations to set aside funding for land acquisition for affordable housing long before a river project begins. The good news is that every neighborhood isn't at high risk of displacement, so it is possible to use the team's needs mapping to target funding available for affordable housing in areas where it is most needed.

+ How does one begin to understand the term "community" in an area of this scale, density, and diversity? How do you know whether you've got everyone at the table?

There are definitely more people at the table than have been included in the past with 41 steering committee members, more than 10 community partner groups, thousands of people that have attended meetings or telephone town halls, and nearly a million people that have interacted digitally, but there is still a need to make the table bigger, particularly as more projects move into implementation. In addition to the diversity of communities along the river there are centuries of cultural histories that are often, and unfortunately, collapsed into a single narrative. This is a mistake. The LA River means many different things to communities along its banks, and those layered cultural meanings create a much richer narrative than many people perceive. Last summer during a Native Communities panel, members of local tribes shared historical and present-day interactions and cultural connections to the river. This panel brought forward some voices that are often overlooked. Another unique event was the LA River Youth Summit in which 800 students from river-adjacent high schools gathered for a day to learn about the river, participate in workshops, and dream about the future of the river. Reimaging the LA River will take decades, and this project is truly generational. Engaging youth to imagine what the river will be is critical.

I don't think that we lose anything when we make the story bigger, when we make room for more narratives. But one thing is clear: the diversity along the LA River means there is not a single solution for the river. Each community has a different set of needs and priorities that must be considered, understood, and integrated into the project design.

+ I know that the design team's community engagement methodology has changed over time. What led to those changes and what strategies have proven most effective? What have you taken away from the public engagement efforts so far?

While the community engagement for the master plan has brought many voices together, we still want to find better ways to authentically engage with a larger cross-section of the communities near the river. Generally speaking, the same 200 people consistently attend river engagement meetings. It's great that this group shows up, but we need to deepen our engagement methods to find ways to reach people beyond the river advocacy groups. We need to talk to people in the adjacent neighborhoods where the impacts of river changes will be felt most strongly. We've heard individuals from some of the most disadvantaged communities note that their voices are not represented often in planning processes. To address this, we have been working to figure out how to ensure the engagement process really engages the community living near a project. On the master plan we have been working with community partners with direct ties to neighborhoods, so that the feedback is an authentic expression of local community. These partner events have been some of the most engaging opportunities for conversation, but we know there is still more to be done to expand engagement. On our new projects near the Rio Hondo Confluence we are working to test a digital engagement tool being developed by River LA based on consumer product research methods that are incentivized to reach a representative demographic in the community directly around the project area. This is exciting because we can quickly get quantitative and qualitative data from a large group of people in the local community through a process that engages digitally with the same volunteers over a period of many months to better understand community needs and desires.

+ It sounds like the process of public engagement, which began with the goal of soliciting public opinions, actually made evident the need to educate communities about a set of varied and sometimes contentious issues. What role does the design team play in this type of outreach?

The educational challenge with the LA River is that most of the time the channel is almost dry, and most people in LA have never seen it at capacity. The small amount of water flowing down the low-flow channel on any given day is primarily treated effluent from wastewater treatment facilities. Most years the rainfall isn't enough to threaten overtopping the levees or channel walls and this lulls river-adjacent communities into a false sense of security. But every few decades a significant rainfall reminds the region that the LA River can dangerously flood, threatening life and property. The river has always flooded, even before there was a single square foot of asphalt in the watershed. In fact, the river sometimes even jumped its banks and found an entirely new route or joined with the San Gabriel River to form a giant water body miles wide. Today, during a 1% annual chance storm event the amount of water that would flow through the river near downtown Los Angeles is around 100,000 cubic feet per second. To put this in perspective, this is more water per second than flows over Niagara Falls.

The biggest issue for us when it comes to talking about the LA River channel is education about the flood conveyance of the river and why it matters. Between now and 2037, LA County has a series of watershed management plan goals to construct over 5,000 acre-feet of storage through low impact development and water quality projects such as green streets, rain gardens, permeable surfaces, and wetlands. These improvements are critical for water quality and small, frequent rainfalls. But during large rainfall events, such as the 1% annual chance storm, the ground saturates, and these water quality projects quickly fill up. Our team studied the impact of watershed imperviousness and found that even if we doubled the goal to 10,000 acre-feet, thereby making the watershed behave as if 50% of the current impervious area was pervious, we would have a minimal effect on peak flows in the LA River.

It takes a minute to take this statistic in. As a landscape architect I want to believe that there is a solution where permeable surfaces make the engineered LA River channel redundant, but it isn't the case. Because housing and development fills the historic floodplain, the river can't be wider without massive displacement, and the idea of planting vegetation within the current river channel width is not possible without significantly increasing flood risk due to friction caused by vegetation.

These concepts are challenging to grasp even for those of us working on this daily. To assist with this education aspect, Geosyntec and OLIN have partnered to make technical, as well as simple, animations showing how water moves through the system. Instead of only seeing graphs and charts, the animations connect hydrographs to illustrative maps and sections that can be watched simultaneously. There are also animations that show how ground becomes saturated during heavier rains and water runs into the LA River channel.

+ What's next?

The LA River Master Plan is only one project we are working on along the LA River. We have several other projects and clients we are collaborating with at river-adjacent sites and many of those projects are moving into concept or schematic design and one is in construction. It is exciting to see progress at many scales along the river. Of course, we are seeking to create multi-benefit projects at an equitable cadence along all 51 miles of the river, and we are heavily focused on connecting to affordable housing policies or preserving existing affordable housing in parallel with new amenities. There are so many projects to do along the LA River that it will take many landscape architects, architects, engineers, and planners working together for the next few decades to create the reimagined river as 51 miles of connected open space.

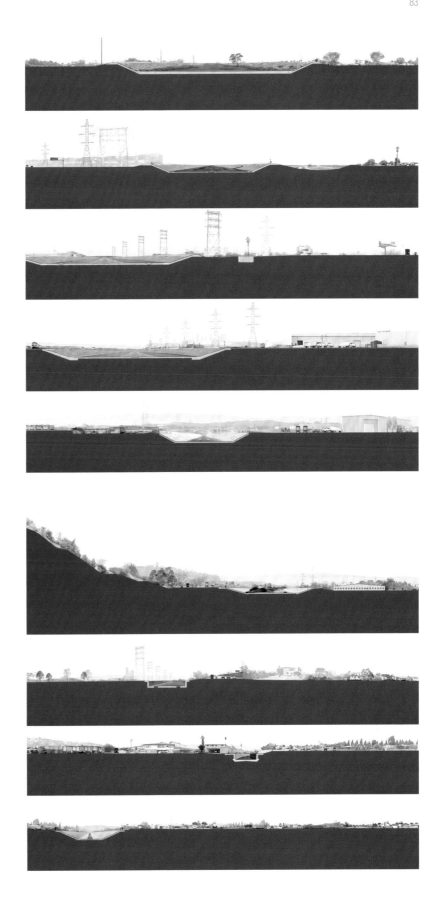

Opposite: Olin's sectional analysis of the LA River.
Above: Scan QR code to watch the *LA River Then and Now* video.

PATTERNS OF BEHAVIOR

CHRILI CAR

Chrili Car leads the landscape department of the Nigerian architecture firm Studio Elementals. His works include interdisciplinary projects in Ghana, where he investigated the migration flows of a settlement being washed away by the sea, and the proxemics patterns of dancers for a new cultural institute; and Austria, where he realized a dementia therapy garden based on the narrative concept of the "hero's journey." Car holds a PhD from the University of Natural Resources and Life Sciences, Vienna, Austria.

+ LANDSCAPE ARCHITECTURE, ECOLOGY, ETHNOGRAPHY

Let's imagine a settlement with a complex parametric layout constructed from renewable materials and consisting of carbon neutral buildings that can be freely adapted to suit changing social and climatic conditions; a place where spatial boundaries do not determine social interaction, but reflect it. Let's call this settlement "Guabuliga." Guabuliga sounds like a utopia created by skilled experts and high-tech software in response to the threat of human self-extinction in the Anthropocene. However, the settlement this article deals with is not part of a utopia, and nor was it designed by professional architects and planners. Guabuliga is real. Its inhabitants built the village in neighborly exchange. In communal meetings the elders decided the rules of spatial developments, and these rules have been passed on orally and refined from one generation to the next. The resulting spatial complexity was the predominant reality in West Africa for centuries.

Guabuliga is a remote village set in the tree savanna of Northern Ghana. The rural parts of West Africa are experiencing rapid social and environmental change, and this led the chief of Guabuliga, in 2012, to invite [applied] Foreign Affairs ([a]FA)—a research lab based at the Institute of Architecture at the University of Applied Arts in Vienna, Austria—to develop a master plan for his community.[1] The interdisciplinary group from the fields of architecture, landscape architecture, and environmental engineering felt that it was first necessary to understand Guabuliga's situation through listening to the community with the intention of investigating sustainable strategies to be developed in collaboration with the inhabitants on site in a second step. What was initially planned as a field trip became, for me, a five-year doctoral project at the University of Natural Resources and Life Sciences in Vienna, Austria,[2] following the method of trailing research. This sort of action research is especially suitable for participatory projects as it is able to adapt to changing situations. While the research questions are clearly defined, the outcomes remain open and reactive. Each new finding influences the selection and procedure of the next inquiry following a circular approach according to phases of listening, conceiving, interacting, and reflecting.[3]

Listen: The Power of Mega-Communities

Fatima and Omu carry buckets and bowls to the school to sell pastries every noon. John weaves baskets under the mango tree in front of his house. When Fatima, Omu, and John are absent, there is nothing more than a tree and its shade in these locations. The young barber Hafiz organizes a dancing competition for teenagers. A private courtyard becom superscript es a disco for an evening. A place becomes a canteen, a workshop, a tailor shop, or an event space with the presence and interaction of people, and its function disappears or changes with their absence.

Listening to the inhabitants of Guabuliga revealed how community has a different meaning in the context of a family-based subsistence economy to the meaning it holds in countries where the division of highly professionalized labor and governmental regulations pervade spatial expressions. Anthropologist Dmitri Bondarenko has referred to traditional West African kingdoms with chieftaincies as "mega-communities," which are non-state societies in spite of the existence of local hierarchical power structures and an overarching national government.[4] Mega-communities are panarchies that consist of self-sufficient groups with personal relations to each other. The members of Guabuliga, for example, are directly related to those who decide the rules of coexistence – their elders.

In Guabuliga the placement of compound houses, the boundaries of protected natural areas, and the borders of districts all depend upon social relations. Because the land is owned communally, it cannot be sold. Families have rights of usage, but when they move away, their land falls back to the community. Instead of fixed demarcations, the six districts of Guabuliga follow family relations as they evolve. If a family member decides not to build close to his or her family but in another part of the village, the house still belongs to the family's district like a satellite within the settlement. Such spatial boundaries are temporary; they do not restrict social coexistence but fluently adapt to social and environmental changes. In one case, due to internal disputes a family divided their compound house like a biological cell. In another, a family relocated their home room by room because an adjacent mango tree grew too big. Such a way of building is reactive: as a family grows, so too does their house. When a house is abandoned, the traditional earth architecture weathers back to the landscape within four years.

Conceive: A Sustainable Vision for a Communal Setting

Communal governance is dominant in Guabuliga, but the village is changing. Young people dream of a contemporary life in the city, and new industrial building materials have become popular. Self-sufficiency is coming to an end with the transition to a market-based economy. When causes and effects become independent from place it poses a challenge for local communal governance, particularly in places where traditional innovation requires generations of gradual change.[5]

Instead of the design response of a master plan, [a]FA collected and merged all these insights to create a sustainable village plan incorporating local best-practices, the activation of urgently needed potentials, and responses to contemporary demands that conflict with traditional practices. The resulting vision features a dry season garden for every family in the riverbed, a greenbelt leading to a new market right in the middle of the village, the re-activation of the water system via a new solar-powered pump, and a concept to address the distribution of infrastructure to decentralized neighborhood clusters without splitting communal land into private parcels.

Interact: A Participatory Greenbelt Project

Guabuliga means "well by the thorn tree." According to its founding myth, hunters settled at the river close to an old thorn tree at the beginning of the 20th century. Today, the river dries annually, the riverine forest has been cut down, and hunting has become insufficient for the local economy as many large animal species have disappeared due to lack of habitat and overhunting. Ghana has the third highest rate of deforestation in West Africa–135,000 hectares of forest disappear every year in the country[6]–and most adults have experienced drastic environmental change during their lifetime. Of all the strategies contained in the sustainable village plan, the community was most interested in the idea of constructing a greenbelt.

Greenbelts are a widely discussed topic in Africa – the Great Green Wall initiative intends to establish a giant greenbelt across the entire African continent in order to prevent a further expansion of the Sahara toward the south.[7] Kenyan environmental activist Wangari Maathai received the Nobel Peace Prize for founding the Green Belt Movement, which plants more than five million trees every year and has caused planting trees to become a symbol of the peaceful fight for democracy in Kenya.[8] Like these initiatives, Guabuliga's greenbelt was also conceived as a community project to achieve ecological restoration, as well as to promote economic independence as the trees provide fruit and medicine.

The realization of the Guabuliga greenbelt was made possible by the collaboration of Guabuliga's residents as local experts with [a]FA, the local NGO Braveaurora, regional institutes for reforestation and ecological farming, and four tree nurseries.[9] Computer-generated density, shadow, and wind studies were augmented with the experiences of local inhabitants with respect to land use patterns and seasonal changes, and, together, local and external participants selected appropriate tree species and chose suitable planting positions on site. The final outcome was an arrangement of trees that reflected the traditional communal organization with its six districts, each represented by their elder at official village councils. Each of the districts received the same number of trees with an equal share of sought-after fruit trees and large autochthonous trees that were vital to ecological restoration, but which the inhabitants usually do not actively grow. After this preparation phase, a festivity took place where the inhabitants planted the 150 trees according to a color code linking suitable species to the selected locations. The greenbelt's maintenance was vested with the community and over time the project became a training area for the local school and a new training garden facilitated education about ecological agriculture and reforestation.

At the core of the greenbelt project was not to simply offer preordained solutions, but to empower local communities to find their own answers. The external professionals acted as advisors and mediators in village meetings, which often lasted several hours. Pluralism and diversity are strong elements of communities and adapting plans to deal with unforeseen challenges is important when working with them: what works well in one group may not work at all in another. Every district, therefore, developed their own system of watering and fencing to care for the trees. Some met in larger groups every week; others distributed certain trees to individual families. One district selected

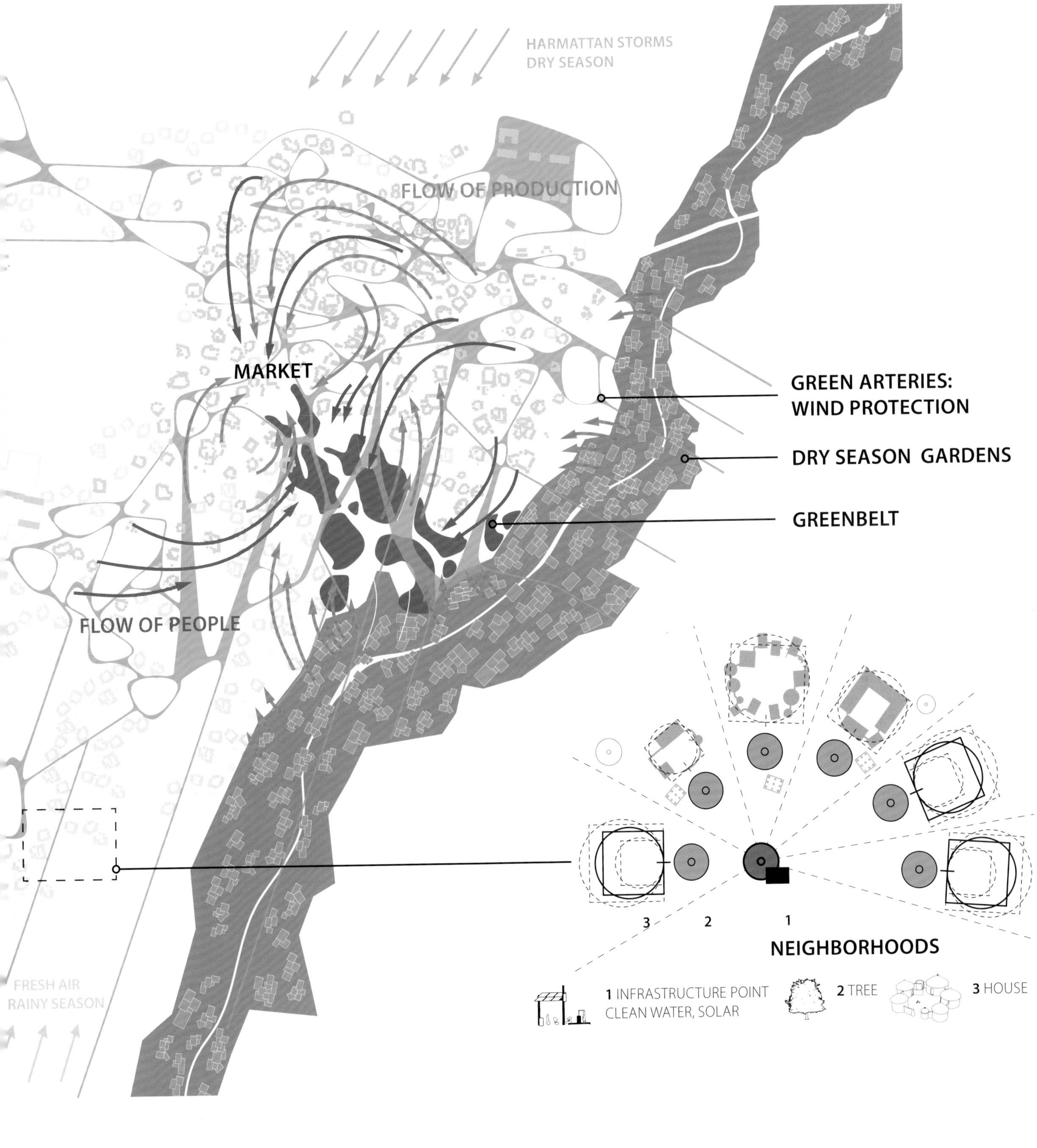

HARMATTAN STORMS
DRY SEASON

FLOW OF PRODUCTION

MARKET

GREEN ARTERIES:
WIND PROTECTION

DRY SEASON GARDENS

GREENBELT

FLOW OF PEOPLE

FRESH AIR
RAINY SEASON

3   2   1

NEIGHBORHOODS

1 INFRASTRUCTURE POINT
CLEAN WATER, SOLAR

2 TREE

3 HOUSE

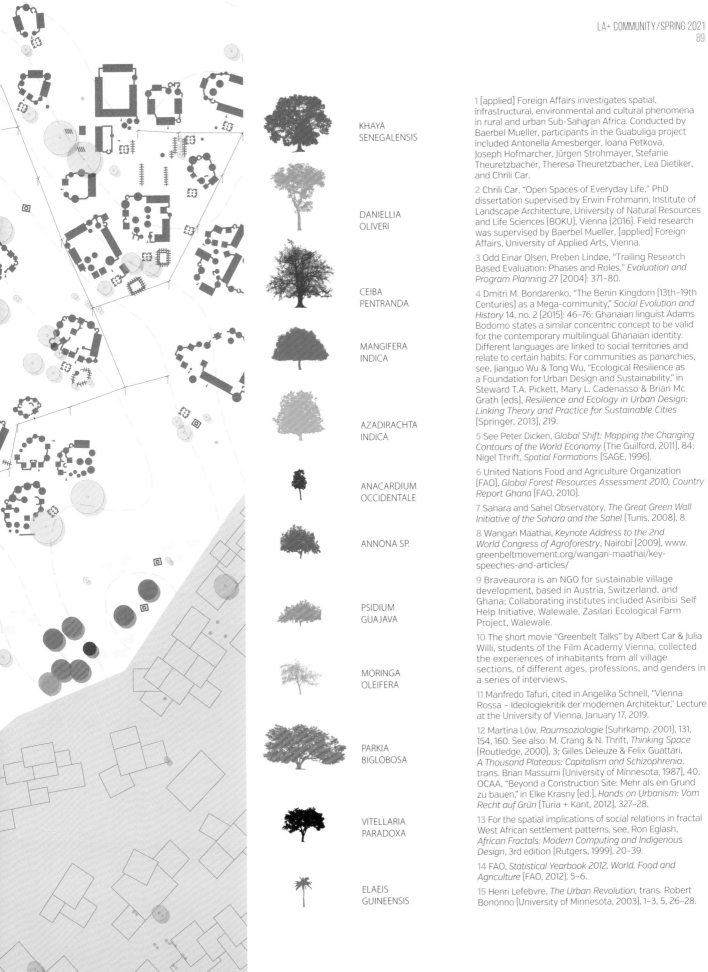

KHAYA
SENEGALENSIS

DANIELLIA
OLIVERI

CEIBA
PENTRANDA

MANGIFERA
INDICA

AZADIRACHTA
INDICA

ANACARDIUM
OCCIDENTALE

ANNONA SP.

PSIDIUM
GUAJAVA

MORINGA
OLEIFERA

PARKIA
BIGLOBOSA

VITELLARIA
PARADOXA

ELAEIS
GUINEENSIS

1 [applied] Foreign Affairs investigates spatial, infrastructural, environmental and cultural phenomena in rural and urban Sub-Saharan Africa. Conducted by Baerbel Mueller, participants in the Guabuliga project included Antonella Amesberger, Ioana Petkova, Joseph Hofmarcher, Jürgen Strohmayer, Stefanie Theuretzbacher, Theresa Theuretzbacher, Lea Dietiker, and Chrili Car.

2 Chrili Car, "Open Spaces of Everyday Life," PhD dissertation supervised by Erwin Frohmann, Institute of Landscape Architecture, University of Natural Resources and Life Sciences (BOKU), Vienna (2016). Field research was supervised by Baerbel Mueller, [applied] Foreign Affairs, University of Applied Arts, Vienna.

3 Odd Einar Olsen, Preben Lindøe, "Trailing Research Based Evaluation: Phases and Roles," *Evaluation and Program Planning* 27 (2004): 371–80.

4 Dmitri M. Bondarenko, "The Benin Kingdom (13th–19th Centuries) as a Mega-community," *Social Evolution and History* 14, no. 2 (2015): 46–76; Ghanaian linguist Adams Bodomo states a similar concentric concept to be valid for the contemporary multilingual Ghanaian identity. Different languages are linked to social territories and relate to certain habits. For communities as panarchies, see, Jianguo Wu & Tong Wu, "Ecological Resilience as a Foundation for Urban Design and Sustainability," in Steward T.A. Pickett, Mary L. Cadenasso & Brian Mc Grath (eds), *Resilience and Ecology in Urban Design: Linking Theory and Practice for Sustainable Cities* (Springer, 2013), 219.

5 See Peter Dicken, *Global Shift: Mapping the Changing Contours of the World Economy* (The Guilford, 2011), 84; Nigel Thrift, *Spatial Formations* (SAGE, 1996).

6 United Nations Food and Agriculture Organization (FAO), *Global Forest Resources Assessment 2010, Country Report Ghana* (FAO, 2010).

7 Sahara and Sahel Observatory, *The Great Green Wall Initiative of the Sahara and the Sahel* (Tunis, 2008), 8.

8 Wangari Maathai, *Keynote Address to the 2nd World Congress of Agroforestry*, Nairobi (2009), www.greenbeltmovement.org/wangari-maathai/key-speeches-and-articles/

9 Braveaurora is an NGO for sustainable village development, based in Austria, Switzerland, and Ghana; Collaborating institutes included Asiribisi Self Help Initiative, Walewale, Zasilari Ecological Farm Project, Walewale.

10 The short movie "Greenbelt Talks" by Albert Car & Julia Willi, students of the Film Academy Vienna, collected the experiences of inhabitants from all village sections, of different ages, professions, and genders in a series of interviews.

11 Manfredo Tafuri, cited in Angelika Schnell, "Vienna Rossa – Ideologiekritik der modernen Architektur," Lecture at the University of Vienna, January 17, 2019.

12 Martina Löw, *Raumsoziologie* (Suhrkamp, 2001), 131, 154, 160. See also: M. Crang & N. Thrift, *Thinking Space* (Routledge, 2000), 3; Gilles Deleuze & Felix Guattari, *A Thousand Plateaus: Capitalism and Schizophrenia*, trans. Brian Massumi (University of Minnesota, 1987), 40; OCAA, "Beyond a Construction Site: Mehr als ein Grund zu bauen," in Elke Krasny (ed.), *Hands on Urbanism: Vom Recht auf Grün* (Turia + Kant, 2012), 327–28.

13 For the spatial implications of social relations in fractal West African settlement patterns, see, Ron Eglash, *African Fractals: Modern Computing and Indigenous Design*, 3rd edition (Rutgers, 1999), 20–39.

14 FAO, *Statistical Yearbook 2012, World, Food and Agriculture* (FAO, 2012), 5–6.

15 Henri Lefebvre, *The Urban Revolution*, trans. Robert Bononno (University of Minnesota, 2003), 1–3, 5, 26–28.

members on a rotating basis in order that all contribute to the project in a fair way.[10]

Reflect: Communities and Professional Expertise

The public is a social ideal and represents an abstraction of humanity as a whole. In contrast, a community is based on direct relationships, which are fundamentally different to the scientific distance of external professionals. Community is a reality of social interaction and not one of paper and pen. Community is about personalities, joint experiences, and immediate actions rather than abstract shapes, bureaucracy, and forward planning. Landscape architecture deals with the design of open spaces, which are often places of social interaction. Top-down designed landscapes are accused of being oppressive, of neglecting those who need open spaces most, of establishing alien normative codes and forcing them onto local communities – in other words, of colonizing space.[11] On this basis, sociologist Martina Löw demanded a fundamentally different understanding when dealing with space suitable for a completely different design practice – one that considers spaces as a relational order of bodies and goods instead of producing them as an absolute frame for social interaction. Spaces should be flexible enough to follow behavior.[12] As plausible as this sounds as a critique, how such relational spaces look or how they can even be produced remains vague.

Communities like Guabuliga show how a relational production of space can work, and how the design of spaces can fluently adapt to social interaction.[13] Forty percent of the global population lives in a communal subsistence economy.[14] Landscape architecture as a profession hardly relates to their existence. The most drastic spatial changes are realized by industries, governments, and communities without the involvement of landscape architects or planners. The discourse about the Anthropocene not only reflects upon the fact that humankind has changed the planet to such an extent that it ceases to provide a habitable home for us, but also upon the impotence of the sciences that made this process possible in the first place. Henri Lefebvre compared this phenomenon with a black box: design professionals know what enters this drastic transformation process, sometimes they see what comes out, but they do not know what happens inside. They may be able to document the process, but they have no plan how to act.[15]

If landscape architects want to overcome their professional blindness, and do not seek to remain a profession for elites, we need to take communal self-organization seriously. For decades, colonialism thought the solutions of self-organized communities to be worthless and that they should follow external expertise instead. Now, its time for the opposite: if we as professionals listen to communities, we can learn from them. The Guabuliga greenbelt project made clear the fine tension between communal self-organization and institutional expertise, but also that these two poles do not necessarily

contradict each other. Communities depend on institutional expertise in times of environmental and cultural shifts, and so do professions. The task of landscape architects is not to take the power of decisions and solutions away from communities, but to empower them to handle challenges on their own, uncover self-determined potentials, provide insights into possibilities, and mediate. When the participants are aware of their roles and communicate them on the same level, the decolonization of mindsets and their spatial manifestations becomes possible, and new kinds of open spaces will emerge. Working with communities is a slow process that needs time to grow. Furthermore, participating professionals need to become familiar in the local social network as personal actors, so that communities can relate to them. This way, landscape architects may not just watch helplessly the drastic transformative processes of the Anthropocene, they will be able to listen to unique local stories and contribute to the continuation of these stories together with local communities.

Previous: Guabuliga greenbelt planting plan.
Left: Guabuliga residents from the short film "Greenbelt Talks" by Albert Car

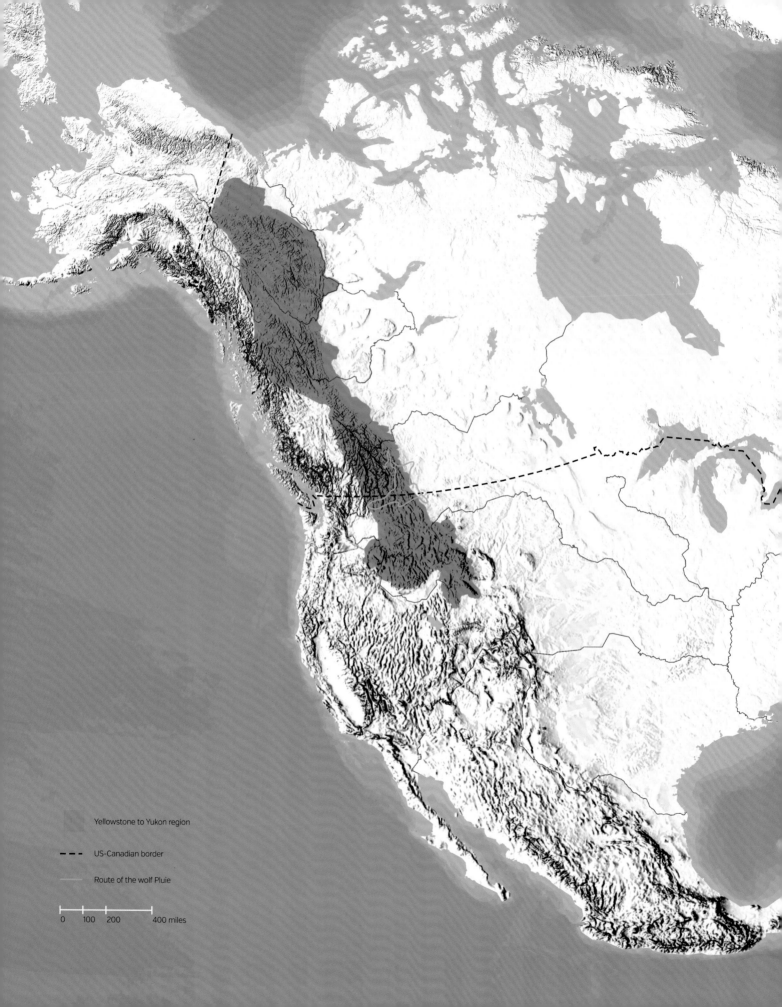

Yellowstone to Yukon region

- - - US-Canadian border

Route of the wolf Pluie

0   100   200   400 miles

IN CONVERSATION WITH
JODI HILTY

Jodi Hilty is a wildlife corridor ecologist and conservation visionary who has focused on using creative, science-based practices to support human and more-than-human life across North American landscapes. In her current role as the President and Chief Scientist of the Yellowstone to Yukon Conservation Initiative (Y2Y), she oversees the implementation of the largest-scale conservation vision on the planet. The accomplishment of the Y2Y vision would see a territory twice the size of Texas reconnected for the vital movement of wildlife and ecosystems in this time of rapid ecological change. Hilty is editor of a number of books that have elevated the importance of ecosystem connectivity, the most recent being the second edition of *Corridor Ecology: Linking Landscapes for Biodiversity Conservation and Climate Adaptation* (2019). **Zuzanna Drozdz** spoke with Hilty to learn more about Y2Y in the context of community.

+ The Y2Y project was started by the conservation community, but it now impacts different communities on the ground. Can you describe this constellation of communities and how the idea of Y2Y was successfully planted among them?

The Yellowstone to Yukon region spans a length of 3,200 km. It's big. When we talk about a single community it does not exist. I would love for all the communities to identify as part of a larger Yellowstone to Yukon community. At this moment though, communities tend to identify with a local place: maybe it's a watershed, maybe it's a town, or maybe it's a group of ranchers across a landscape.

There are over 70 traditional territories and associated communities of indigenous people across the Yellowstone to Yukon region that are really important in terms of both the history and the current living individuals in the region. There are also what we call classic resort communities, places like Banff National Park in Canada and Jackson Hole in Wyoming. Only a small group of people live there but millions of people pass through. In addition to that, there are what we call ranching communities, generally based in the mountain valleys. They often have large pieces of land and are responsible for stewarding public lands where they graze their cattle. Then there are urban communities – places like Boise, Idaho or Bozeman, Montana. Many people who move to these communities are drawn there for nature-based recreation. We see a lot of businesses that are relocating there for the quality of life, which they see as a potential plus for their employees. We also see an increasing baby boomer retirement community. In fact, the number one source of income in the greater Yellowstone ecosystem is non-source income, such as trust funds and retirement investment incomes. A lot of these people are not actively ranching or living in urban communities. Their ideal is to live right on the edge of public lands. They are literally buying up pieces of nature for their retirement. These are some of the diverse kinds of communities within the Yellowstone to Yukon region.

+ What roles has the Y2Y Conservation Initiative played in engaging these various communities to build the coalition across the region that is necessary to implement such a large vision?

As an organization, Y2Y is just 25 people and so we work primarily through partner organizations. There are some places where we're really on the ground and in the community, but you can think of us more as the general contractor.

If we need to get wildlife from one mountain range to another across private lands, and we don't want to see those lands subdivided—because that could be the death knell for that being a functional corridor—we might work with a series of different land trusts. The land trusts then engage directly with the agricultural or ranching communities. When it comes to working, for example, on wildlife road crossings, we engage with lots of different partners: sometimes businesses, sometimes other nonprofits, and sometimes local communities. Whether we take the lead on working with a local community or others do depends on the capacity of the region. We're really trying to empower local groups, including volunteer groups. For example, we have a

community on Highway 3–the first east–west road north of the US border in Canada–where the community is actually collecting the data before overpasses and underpasses go in to look at effectiveness levels. They are really the on-the-ground folks in that region.

We have also been working with Treaty 8 First Nations in northeastern British Columbia. Right now there is a proposed agreement between these First Nations, the Canadian federal government, and the British Columbia provincial government that will create a caribou protection area that will be an indigenous led conservation area. We have been working with that community for 10 years to support a shared vision of their territory being better protected. Less than 4% of the landscape is protected in this area, and some argue that it is more industrialized than the oil sands in Alberta. From a Y2Y perspective it is the narrowest part of the Yellowstone to Yukon region. In this case, the First Nations are the ones at the negotiating table and our job is to support them. There is a fair amount of racism associated with these First Nations actually getting their treaty rights, which include the ability to hunt caribou. These communities have forgone hunting since the 1990s because the caribou herds have tanked because of industrial development. How do we help them recover a species that is culturally important? We have a shared vision. We support them on pushing the government and we help them in getting other voices to support them against local loud voices that are afraid of this change.

+ What was the original narrative of Y2Y so as to communicate the larger vision to different constituencies?

I think that one of the greatest strengths of Y2Y is the vision to connect and protect one of the most intact mountain ecosystems in the world so that both people and nature can thrive. Since the beginning we have seen that people think this is an audacious vision. Y2Y was actually featured on *The West Wing* as a "wingnut idea!" What's really exciting is that through the power of this shared vision, we have made significant progress toward conserving this place. Despite the fact that people are moving there in droves and there is pressure for natural resource development, we are making progress, and that's really exciting. It is the power of helping communities take control of what they love about living in the Yellowstone to Yukon region, about living in the Rockies. Our job as the group that keeps that vision of the 3,200 km corridor alive is to make sure that folks who care about what's going on in their backyard are prioritizing things like connectivity that matter both locally and at that large scale.

The conservation paradigm in the 20th century was focused on protecting certain areas that are important to the conservation of biodiversity, but they alone are not adequate. That is why we have to think about connectivity. We

often tell stories through either the eyes of wildlife or through people's experience. There is the story of Pluie, the wolf that ranged 100,000 km² over 30 different jurisdictions, two countries, three states, two provinces and was ultimately legally killed with her pups in British Columbia. She was symbolic of the fact that we create political lines on maps and wildlife don't know about them. We can also talk about Karsten Heuer, a former leader of the Yellowstone to Yukon Conservation Initiative, who in his early days actually hiked the whole thing to understand what it looks like and feels like.

+ A lot of indigenous groups have origin stories and cosmologies with strong spiritual links to wildlife. How do these different ontologies or cosmologies shape the relationship that you build with those groups or the ways in which you try to support them?

We talk about this a lot in Canada, that there is Western scientific information and that there is traditional knowledge – the understanding and cumulative body of knowledge, know-how, and understanding from peoples with extended histories of cultural traditions and interaction with the natural environment. What is important for Y2Y is that both kinds of information are equally valid and can help advance shared values across the Yellowstone to Yukon region. I recently met with Loren Bird Rattler, who is a Blackfoot from northwestern Montana and part of a number of wider initiatives including the Innii Initiative. *Innii* means bison in Blackfoot. To the Blackfeet, bison are the center of the world. The Blackfeet are a people divided across the US–Canada border. Their vision for bison restoration is to bring bison back into the landscape. For them, it's not just about putting bison out on the landscape it's about ecosystem health as a metaphor for their people and restoring the wellness of their people. It's about what they're eating. It's about making sure that their grandchildren understand the connection they have with this magnificent animal. It's also about their economy; the reality is that in today's world they, like everyone else, need to have sources of income and livelihood. So this large initiative—at the center of which is the bison—seeks to help in all these different ways. I think that is an incredibly powerful story and a microcosm of what Y2Y envisions as success where both nature and people are doing well together.

+ You mentioned that this is one of the last remaining intact mountain ecosystems on the planet. How does the concept of intactness relate to the concept of community?

Well there are two ways we can talk about intactness. There is ecological intactness, which is about the ecological communities being largely intact. That means that one could look at what kinds of wildlife and vegetation existed pre-European colonization and find those elements still present in the Yellowstone to Yukon region. Ecological processes like fire, flooding, and predator–prey dynamics also continue to exist across a lot of that region.

Then we can talk about human communities and intactness. Human communities in the region have traditionally been quite small. It is a hard

place to eke out a living, particularly if you're living off the land. So it has been largely left alone ecologically. That said, I think that we have been undergoing a rapid transition like the rest of the world. There is natural resource extraction, mega-mining, and logging increasingly impacting the landscape. And now we also have mobile human communities who are looking to have second homes. They are looking for quality of life, and one of the places they can achieve that is in this Rocky Mountain region of Yellowstone to Yukon. It's sheer numbers, but it's also sprawling development. It's important to plan communities so that people and nature can thrive.

+ Have there been any groups or individuals that have felt alienated by the Y2Y initiative, or that have opposed Y2Y in some way, and if so how have you negotiated that?

That is an ongoing effort. There are groups that occasionally bump up against the Y2Y vision. Let's start at the big scale. The Yellowstone to Yukon Initiative is a big umbrella group; we will partner with any group that we can find a shared vision with. For example, we work with some of the humane society groups that are supporting national-level wildlife corridor legislation in the United States. We also work with the hunting and trapping community, who are some of the best on-the-ground naturalists in the region and whose livelihoods are dependent on wildlife. These two groups really don't always see eye-to-eye and they will often criticize Y2Y as being one or the other when we're really neither.

We also face criticism from the off-road-vehicle and motorized recreation communities that really love nature and love to get out there. We're not against motorized recreation; however, it is a challenge to maintain motorized recreation in a sustainable way when local populations and numbers of visitors are growing. In some places you can go anywhere in your off-road vehicle, and you can open-access-camp anywhere, and it's having an impact. When there was just one million people in Alberta, the impact was a lot smaller. Now that there are four times as many people in Alberta, and even more visiting than ever before, that landscape is much more impacted. So, we work to support the government to make decisions that ensure that all the different kinds of recreation can be out there in the future, but that the landscape is managed with the large landscape connectivity vision and long-term ecological value in mind. There are groups that say, "I just want to make sure my kids can do what I did when I was young," not recognizing that the world has really changed.

When we address issues around logging companies or forestry efforts, people are worried that we're going to close down their community. Yet when we are living with the legacy of the short-term benefits of past over-logging, and really not having enough, does that mean that they should have the right to log the last of the old growth? Well, no, but then the conservation

community looks like the bad guys when it was former policy decisions that enabled an unsustainable amount of yield. It's about coming to the table and talking about what a green economy looks like that can be sustained into the long term and how it can provide for those communities. But it's a scary thing for those communities to be regulated when they haven't been subject to regulation previously.

+ Are there ways that you have found that are productive to think about what can be done to support those communities struggling with maintaining livelihoods and meeting conservation goals right now?

It was really cool to see a report last year that Colorado is trying to grab every bit of open space and keep it open because they have done economic analyses that show the value of open space to their economy. It's about attracting businesses that can employ local people, it's about attracting a tourism-based economy, and it's about quality of life issues.

Right now at Y2Y we're supporting economic analyses in places where we're not sure that the forestry has been sustainable in order to provide information on the numbers about short-term gain versus long-term gain. A lot of this is driven by the short terms that politicians sit in office and their desire to get returns to their communities quickly. If you were to look at the economics within a four-year period, the construction of a sprawling development pays off. If you look at it for a 50-year period for that community, however, it is going to cost that community a tremendous amount of money to sustain. That's not often on the table for discussion, and the communities don't see it. Likewise, when you think of things like fracking, and what we see is boom-bust communities. Those are not always thriving communities in the Yellowstone to Yukon region. Are those the kind of communities that we want to see in the long term and where families want to raise their kids? We need to look beyond that four-year political horizon.

+ How have people responded to the idea and reality of rewilding efforts with animals that might be perceived as threatening— such as grizzly bears and wolverines—in proximity to their communities?

It's interesting; I would say it is a mixed bag. Grizzly bears in the greater Yellowstone ecosystem have come back from the very brink of extinction. When I was a kid there were just a couple of dozen grizzlies in Yellowstone National Park, and now they have spilled beyond. Likewise, with the successful reintroduction of wolves in the area. There were significant ecological impacts of wolves missing from the ecosystem. Yet to criticize the conservation community for a moment, I don't think we fully grasped how successful we would be. Some people think it is a great thing: watching wildlife in Yellowstone and in the greater region is a multi-million-dollar industry. At the same time there are animals spilling beyond the boundaries not only of Yellowstone National Park but throughout the greater Yellowstone region onto ranches and into communities. It has caused both perceived

and real hardships. I think the conservation community—meaning natural resource agencies and conservation NGOs—have been struggling to support ranching communities that never before had to live with these large toothy carnivores, and that therefore do not have the tools and the resources to coexist with them.

One of the things that Y2Y does in response is to support local community coexistence programs. This might mean putting out a range rider – a person on a horse hanging out with the cows all summer long. Because large carnivores tend to avoid people, the idea is that a person out there might deter the toothy carnivores. We're supporting some research out of the University of Wisconsin to test this technique because it's increasingly used and it's expensive, so we really want to know that it's effective. We have been supporting a number of different carcass composting efforts, helping ranchers get these dead animals off of the landscape and composted so large carnivores are not eating them and developing a taste for them. We're not the only group that does this. It's exciting to see so many groups that are working to reduce conflicts, and my hope is that over the long term the Y2Y communities that do live with these toothy animals do so with pride. In the United States, this is the last part of the lower 48 states that has these large carnivores, particularly grizzly bears. It's amazing to get to live with them, but there are also hardships. So, we need to recognize both and hopefully get to a point where we are celebrating those ranchers who are able to both successfully husband their animals and to coexist with these carnivores. These agriculturalists, these ranchers, are the ones with these large open spaces that really provide a buffer to our public lands.

+ Are there still debates in the scientific community regarding the benefits and drawbacks of ecological connectivity?

When working on an updated version of a book, *Corridor Ecology*, we reviewed the literature and I think increasingly the debate is done. A meta-analysis of corridors and their effectiveness concludes that while not all of the efforts to create corridors have necessarily been as successful as their stated intentions, when you look at all of the corridor efforts, they are in fact increasing connectivity—genetic connectivity, population connectivity, demographic connectivity—and benefiting overall biodiversity. I think there are always the outside critiques, but so far, we haven't seen a study saying corridors are bad. The meta-advice is if we want to conserve biodiversity in this time of climate change, and generally, we really have to think about connectivity.

Connectivity can be really small or it can be really large. We're helping a small group in British Columbia trying to make sure that western toads don't get smushed in the road. Simple construction interventions keep the toads off the road by making sure there are underpasses that they can use without dying, to get from where they reproduce to where they spend their winters. Then there is the large scale, like wolverines moving over mega-distances; a viable population of wolverines in the US Rockies requires that they stay connected to Canada, because there are really only maybe 150 to 200 wolverines in the US Rockies, and that's the maximum there will be. A viable population needs to be much bigger than that, so maintaining that connectivity into Canada and with the population there is what a true sustainable population will look like.

+ If we think for a moment about Y2Y as a giant experiment of unprecedented scale, what have been some of the things that you've learned—either from your own research or your review of the field—that changed how you think about assembling wildlife corridors in the Yellowstone to Yukon region and beyond?

First, I will say that at right around the time that Y2Y was being created there were also other very large landscape initiatives getting going. The Paseo Pantera in Latin America was coming out at that time as well. There are a number of new findings out there that are really important. One of them is we can't necessarily account for every single species. Robin Steenweg's research shows that grizzly bears are a pretty good umbrella species. What I mean is that if you get the protected areas and connectivity right for grizzly bears, you get it right for a lot of other animals. That's important because it's really hard if you're trying to track every individual in every single direction.

Another piece of it is the uneasy challenge that national parks have been up against for a long time. National parks are simultaneously for the enjoyment of people and the conservation of biodiversity, and that's an uneasy tension as we start to get millions and millions of people coming into Banff, Waterton, Glacier, and Grand Teton National Parks. How do we make sure that people can get into these parks, because connecting with nature is so important? What I often say is that people love nature and the fact that these parks are overflowing with people means that we need more of them. We need more places where we're helping guide people into nature in a way that is sustainable and inspiring people to care about nature.

When we wrote the first edition of *Corridor Ecology* in 2007, there were really no papers about connectivity and climate change. When we were writing the new version that came out this year, there were 183 papers on connectivity and climate change alone. And while we knew connectivity was important before that evidence, there is new impetus showing that if we want species to survive and move across the landscape, we need to create space amongst the sea of humanity and all of its developments and activities.

Another issue that has really come to a head is how much of a genetic barrier roads can be, and we're seeing this, for example, in research showing that what was once a continuous genetic population of grizzly bears, is now in pockets that are genetically differentiated and the lines around

them are roads. It's not just grizzly bears: we see this for wolverines, we see this for mountain goats. The major roads are a genetic barrier for many animals and roads are just getting busier and bigger. Ideally, in the Yellowstone to Yukon region we're going to deal with them now, today, so that we don't end up in the situation of Los Angeles where they're building a 55-million-dollar overpass over a 10-lane highway. That's incredible and I'm so appreciative that the LA community cares enough about wildlife to do that. But we have the opportunity to learn earlier, to do it right earlier, to avoid the predicament of having to fix it in hindsight.

+ So, what's the future for Y2Y?

Our hope and vision is that people living within the communities of the Yellowstone to Yukon region and people around the world recognize and celebrate that this is one of the most intact ecosystems in the world and work together to keep it that way.

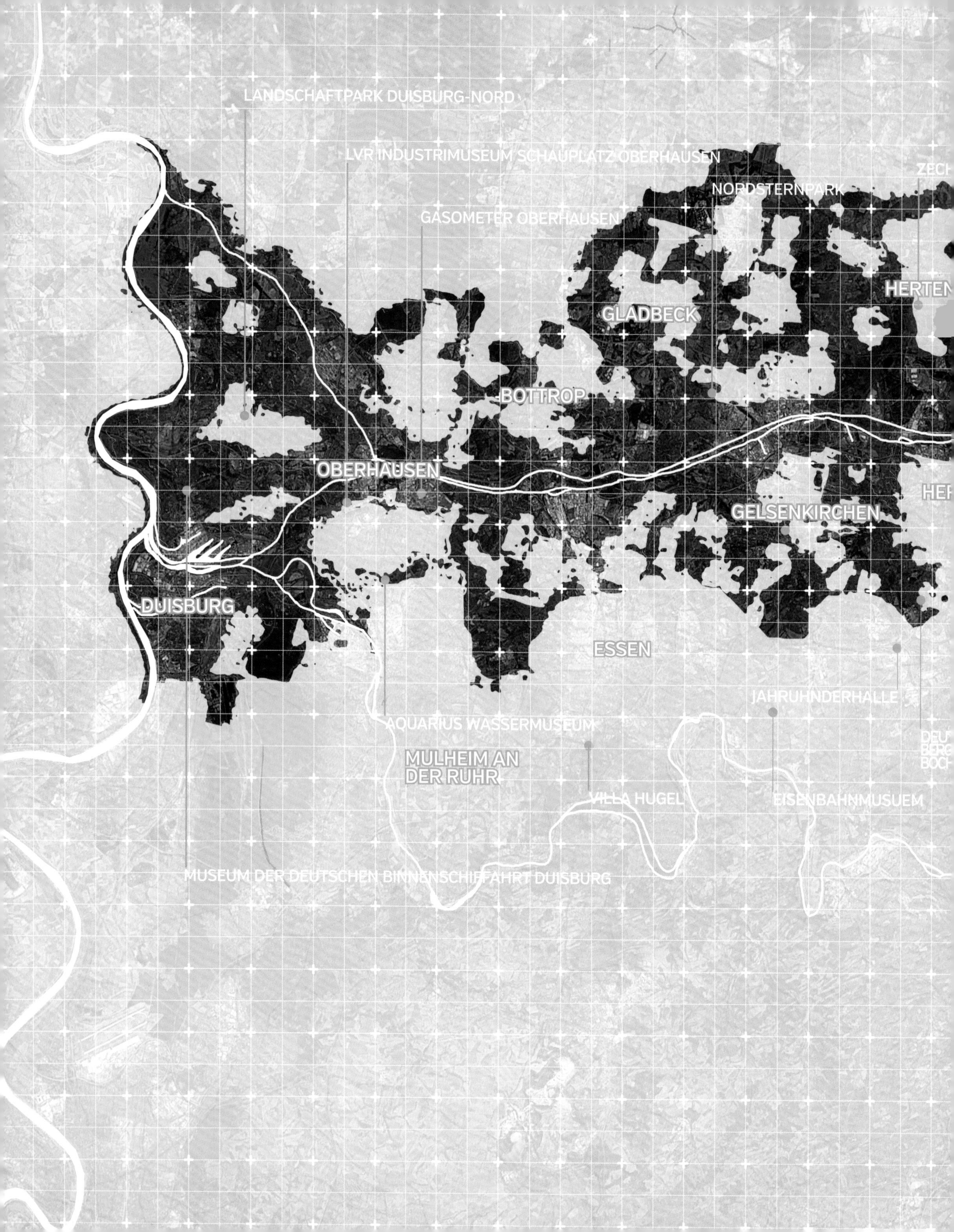

LANDSCHAFTPARK DUISBURG-NORD

LVR INDUSTRIMUSEUM SCHAUPLATZ OBERHAUSEN

NORDSTERNPARK

ZECH

GASOMETER OBERHAUSEN

HERTEN

GLADBECK

BOTTROP

OBERHAUSEN

GELSENKIRCHEN

HER

DUISBURG

ESSEN

JAHRUHNDERHALLE

AQUARIUS WASSERMUSEUM

DEU
BERG
BOCH

MULHEIM AN
DER RUHR

VILLA HUGEL

EISENBAHNMUSUEM

MUSEUM DER DEUTSCHEN BINNENSCHIFFAHRT DUISBURG

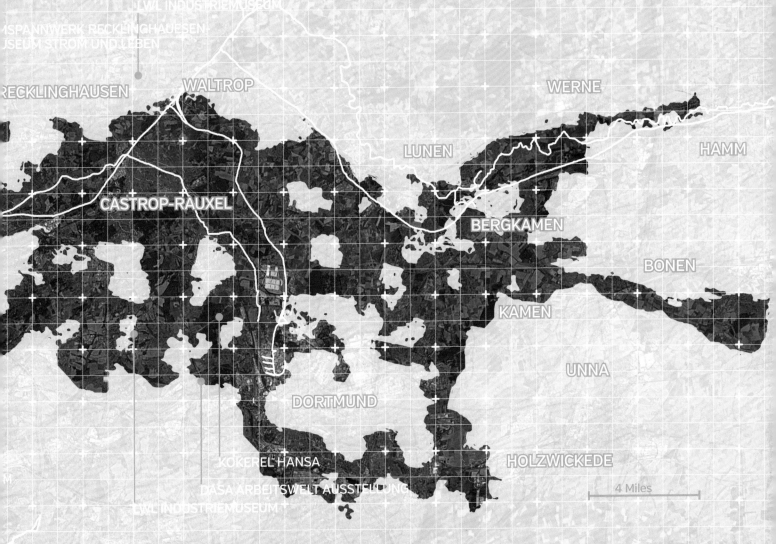

LWL INDUSTRIEMUSEUM

UMSPANNWERK RECKLINGHAUSEN
MUSEUM STROM UND LEBEN

RECKLINGHAUSEN

WALTROP

WERNE

HAMM

LUNEN

CASTROP-RAUXEL

BERGKAMEN

BONEN

KAMEN

UNNA

DORTMUND

HOLZWICKEDE

KOKEREL HANSA

DASA ARBEITSWELT AUSSTELLUNG

LWL INDUSTRIEMUSEUM

4 Miles

IN CONVERSATION WITH

MICHAEL SCHWARZE-RODRIAN

From the ruins of World War II, the coal miners and steel workers of the Ruhr region rebuilt West German industry. For the children of this post-war generation, however, the stability and identity of a working-class community would–by the 1980s–prove elusive. As mineral resources were exhausted and labor markets globalized, it became clear that the communities of the Ruhr would have to reinvent themselves if they were to survive. In what seemed at first an unlikely vision, Germany's engine room would now become its park. The transformation of the Ruhr from industrial ruins to vibrant cultural landscape is a remarkable story of planning, politics, and community coalescing around a clear landscape architectural vision. To understand how this project unfolded and how it continues to evolve **Erica Yudelman** interviewed Michael Schwarze-Rodrian, former Director of European and Regional Networks Ruhr, on behalf of LA+.

+ Emscher Landscape Park covers an extensive region known as the Ruhr in northwest Germany. Can you set the scene for LA+ readers by briefly describing the region's industrial history, its urban fabric, and its landscape condition?

The Emscher River and its tributaries and the Emscher Landscape Park are located in the northern part of the center of the Ruhr in Germany. This area suffered greatly from the decline of the coal and steel industries since the 1960s and was thought of as poor, polluted, and without a future. The story of Ruhr is one of a group of independent cities going through shared, simultaneous, and comprehensive transformation to address the structural changes needed to replace old heavy industries reliant on coal and steel to a diverse, service-based and knowledge-based economy.

The massive green and blue investments that have been undertaken in the last 30 years and that are still ongoing are part of a new perspective of an intelligent, sustainable, just, and integrated Metropolitan Region Ruhr with a total population of 5.1 million. The Emscher Landscape Park is a 457 km2 regional park system between 20 cities, which includes seven north–south oriented regional corridors (where the tributaries of the Emscher River system flow) and an east–west corridor named New Emscher Valley. The park operates across three spatial and political levels: the first is the regional park and its network of bike paths; the second is the seven inter-municipal working groups, which are responsible for seven green-belt corridors; and the third is over 100 site-specific local design projects, which concern the conversion of the former coal and steel industries and their transport infrastructures into ecologically restored and socially activated spaces.

+ Central to the transformation of this area was the restoration of the waterways – can you explain how this was achieved?

We've been working on the restoration of the Emscher River system for the past 30 years in parallel with the development of parks, and this work is ongoing. The Emscher River and its tributaries have been converted from concrete open wastewater channels into natural stream systems. For this, a new 423 km underground sewer network was constructed to separate waste and river water. Subsequently, the concrete was removed and the channelization reversed by widening the stream profiles. A system of floodplains and near-natural retention reservoirs provide flood protection. The morphology and connectivity of the Emscher and its tributaries were then restored aboveground, covering a total length of 341 km. This complete conversion of the whole Emscher River system enhances the quality of life and the

+ During your talk at the 2019 Design with Nature Now event in Philadelphia, you mentioned that the first reaction to the Emscher Landscape Park planning feasibility study in 1988 was ridicule. Can you explain the attitude that the governments and residents of the area had at first and how it evolved over time?

+ With such a large project area, your team has had to deal with many different communities of interest including residents, governments, and industries. What methods did you use to engage with these stakeholder communities and what did you learn from them?

ecological environment along the rivers, as well as in the urban neighborhoods. The wastewater-free Emscher system will be completed by 2021 and the last aboveground works on the riverbeds and banks will be finished around 2025.

The common opinion back in 1988 when we started was that "landscape" and "beauty" are outside, somewhere else – not in the heart of an old industrial region. Even though we had discovered and mapped many vacant and potential sites for a new urban landscape development nobody could imagine it. There were no precedents showing that industrial wasteland could be both beautiful and useful. The decision-makers in the region–in the cities and in the state government, as well as the users of the new parks–had to be convinced project by project. Year-by-year, as more projects were completed, anxieties abated.

Building regional consensus and inter-municipal partnerships was, and still is, the essence of the Emscher Landscape Park's success. Planning negotiations have to happen at all levels of society to stimulate and produce continuity for the park's development. Politicians, as well as private stakeholders, interest groups, environmentalists, unions, and NGOs were all involved in the process. Architects, water management experts, biologists, ecologists, landscape architects, city planners, artists, and the media were invited to develop solutions for particular sites in the park or along the river.

It was important that the transformation of the urban landscape was linked to the cultural identity of the region and the local cities and towns, and that local people were engaged in the process of change. The local authorities for environment, city planning, business development, and local companies supported custom-made solutions for local needs. Unique site-specific projects were generated as a result of this engagement–parks, art installations, event and exhibition spaces, bikeways, and new ecologies–which had high impact and connected directly with different communities. This strategy of broad engagement through a flexible planning system with a project-by-project approach holds good today, particularly in a time of increasingly complex funding arrangements.

+ The postindustrial nature theme of Emscher Landscape Park embraces a wild aesthetic with some plants that are seen as invasive. Was this approach controversial?

+ For over three decades, you and your colleagues have successfully stewarded a complicated planning process to create a vast regional greenspace system. What do you think has been the key to that success?

No, or only to some ecological experts. During our ongoing ecological survey about the industrial biotopes, species, and qualities since the beginning of the 1990s we discovered the beauty and importance of the many neophytes that came to the Ruhr with the trains of heavy industries over the past 150 years.

A typical challenge for all long-duration projects like Emscher Landscape Park is the turnover of decision-makers, stakeholders, and political trends during the development and construction period. To reduce the risk of interruptions it was necessary to stay flexible, to be open and transparent, to integrate new stakeholders, and to continually show the ongoing benefits of the park. Transformation at this scale takes many years so it is also necessary and desirable to reassess progress and priorities at regular intervals to refresh proposals and reengage political support and funding.

I think strategic and voluntary cooperation on a regional and local level, politically and technically, was also essential to realizing the vision and to delivering the regional park system we see today. Cooperation is based on trust built up over time through careful moderation and inclusive management. Such cooperation is unlikely to work without the capacity to build on different capabilities and interests in space and time, and this requires long-term revenue investment in core teams, not just in capital projects.

Significant public intervention was needed in the first 30 years of the initiative to deliver change such that the private sector felt able to come on board and begin to make investments in the area. Sound investment in quality projects has set a standard that continues to be met regardless of current issues and politics. The Ruhr has a reputation for quality in strategies, programs, and projects – people now expect this and the investment is recouped in economic, cultural, and environmental benefits. Finally, an important factor in the park's success was the unique amount of brownfields we had to start with. On the one hand it presented a big challenge with respect to ecological restoration, but on the other it has given the park its enduring character.

Opposite: The Ruhr region's post-industrial landscape now hosts a wide variety of connected parks featuring event and recreation spaces, cultural institutions, and public artworks.

IN CONVERSATION WITH KATE

ORFF ▷

Kate Orff is founder and principal of SCAPE Studio and the first landscape architect to be awarded a prestigious MacArthur Foundation Fellowship. She is also the director of the Urban Design Program and co-director of the Center for Resilient Cities and Landscapes at Columbia University's Graduate School of Architecture, Planning, and Preservation. SCAPE Studio utilizes research- and practice-based approaches to design, conceptualizing environments as complex socio-ecological places and broadening prior definitions of the profession as a whole. Its projects, such as the "Living Breakwaters" response to Hurricane Sandy and the "Oyster-tecture" proposal for Gowanus Canal, illustrate Orff's vision for landscape design: integrating with an environment's natural processes, enhancing its essential functions, and communicating its significance to vulnerable communities reliant upon it. **Claire Napawan** discussed with her the significance of community—and all the diverse interpretations of the term—within her work.

+ In the introduction to your book *Toward an Urban Ecology*, you describe its goal as being "to reconceive urban landscape design as a form of activism." How are you employing your studio's work as activism? What specific projects have accomplished this role, and what were the concrete results?

Well, for starters, activism in the context of design often does not take the same form as it does on a broader political stage. I can participate as an individual in the Climate March, or donate to election candidates, or support grassroots movements and serve on non-profit boards, but that's different than a stance of activism as a practice, which has defined SCAPE's approach to landscape. Much of our "activist" practice has taken the form of asking new questions, which were not part of a traditional approach to landscape architecture. For example, back around 2004, I was active in the New York City Audubon Society and participated in Project Safe Flight, which was a group of volunteers picking up neo-tropical migrant birds from the bases of glass buildings. After a few meetings, it became apparent that I should be using my skills in mapping, writing, and design rather than picking up dead birds. One of life's more heartbreaking moments is to hold a bright yellow warbler that has flown thousands of miles, at the base of the most generic apartment building. So I worked with the director to submit a grant application to the US Fish and Wildlife Service to develop bird-safe building guidelines as a handbook for architects, building managers, and others to make minor changes to prevent the biological, and often unseen, carnage. These guidelines won an American Society of Landscape Architecture Award (ASLA) in 2008, were incorporated into the American Bird Conservancy document, and have been implemented in buildings and landscapes worldwide. That's just one example of seeking out new questions that impact the landscape more broadly that don't have a clear response. Beyond that, on almost every project we do, we try to expand the brief to include habitat restoration and work that directly addresses the climate crisis. For example, for a waterfront park in San Francisco, China Basin Park, we've spent a lot of time developing a series of tidal shelves for intertidal and subtidal habitat; expanding the "client group" to include non-human species and systems; and letting design be guided by the best available science in addition to aesthetic and civic value.

+ You've stated that community engagement has forced you, as a landscape architect, "to grapple with the knowledge that there is no single problem and thus no single solution that could make a sufficient difference." Can you elaborate on this and how it supports the argument for increased community engagement within landscape architecture practice?

I learned a lot from my early mapping and writing on Jamaica Bay about the nested challenges underpinning climate change and the layers of regulation and governance and implementation complexity that hits from so many different angles – environmental, social, and economic. In 2005, Jamaica Bay was a sort of harbinger of environmental collapse and sea-level rise. The future of the bay is intimately tied to the joint water- and sewer-shed outside its official boundaries. For me, this was a moment of complete reorientation, a deep understanding that to design the landscape at a scale that I was interested in–the regional ecosystem scale–is essentially a social project and, moreover, a communications project. I've carried this lesson with me ever since and every SCAPE project has a unique communications underpinning, whether that's intense on-the-ground community "river paddles" or meetings in high school auditoriums, to handbooks, websites, and other, more flexible tools.

Substantive–not perfunctory–community engagement is one of the most important aspects of this process. It's the means by which the multi-disciplinary teams we work on can communicate, at the outset, the logic driving different design scenarios to a general audience and build public and private support around projects. Done correctly, this is both a public service that meets people where they are and speaks directly to their experiences with climate change (whether or not they call it that) and a tool to empower existing leaders embedded within communities to become champions for more equitable climate adaptation. The community engagement process should not just extract lessons learned from communities and inject them into plans destined to gather dust on a shelf, without any actionable or fundable implementation strategy – they should build on physical coalitions that already exist, mobilize people, and direct investment back into the frontline communities that will be most impacted.

+ Community activism proved to be an important catalyst to the design process and the success of your Living Breakwaters response for the 2016 Rebuild by Design competition. Can you describe that process and how it may have differed from previous projects you and your studio had tackled in the past?

The fact that the Rebuild by Design process asked so much of its proponents in terms of community outreach and coalition-building was one of several key determinants for the advancement and ability to secure funding for all of the projects. Again, this is a very different process – not just asking people to respond to a project with a specific spatial envelope (a new waste treatment plan, for example), but to engage in discussions around risk and resilience more broadly. Engagement required for Rebuild by Design was condensed within a single year; and since we began to lead the Living Breakwaters project through implementation with the NY Governor's Office of Storm Recovery, it has extended far beyond that. The tools required for engagement around a project like Living Breakwaters were entirely novel: educational partnerships, "shore tours" and experiential engagement at local festivals, new kinds of models and exhibits. Conducting outreach in elementary, middle, and high schools–in particular, forming a partnership with the New York Harbor School and now the Billion Oyster Project–was a key aspect. Working alongside young people learning the value of harbor restoration, oyster gardening was a way to build a multi-generational public coalition around the project while communicating both the risks of climate change and the opportunities of living infrastructure and landscapes.

+ Engaging communities meaningfully sometimes requires new forms of communication. "Safari 7" is an example of one of your early projects that tested this approach. Can you describe this project and how you translated the landscape design process into the design of community-based communication?

I initiated Safari 7 as part of the Urban Landscape Lab at Columbia Graduate School of Architecture, Planning, and Preservation with Janette Kim and Glen Cummings. It was also the answer to a question which had to do with awareness and love of the urban landscape in all of its quirkiness – abandoned lots, falcons in parks, the ecological value of cemeteries. It was initiated as a podcast based on interviews that transformed the number 7 subway line in New York into a sort of urban safari line and then expanded into a multimedia and experiential engagement tool with a physical model, drawings as part of a traveling exhibit, and other audio-visual elements. Safari 7 was conceived when the word "podcast" was new, and we used this form to engage participants as contributors rather than passive observers or suppliers of information: "Safari 7 imagines train cars as eco-urban classrooms and invites travelers to act as park rangers in their city." Its primary purpose is education, but it also allows individuals to layer on their own nuances and understandings of how urban and ecological systems interact and create productive friction. We all learned a lot from Safari 7, plus it was just a lot of fun to work on! Later, we adapted the lessons from Safari 7 into the SCAPE context in a range of different ways to inform our engagement events and programming.

+ While much of your recent practice has focused on New York, you've done a number of projects in other parts of the US, such as the Chattahoochee River Greenway in Atlanta, GA and the McCoy's Creek Restoration in Jacksonville, FL. How do you overcome the challenges of working within a community that is not your own? Are there different methods you employ when engaging with new communities?

We've been working on a cluster of soft-bottom watercourse restoration projects in the Southeast, including the McCoy's Creek Restoration and Recreation Plan in Jacksonville and now the Bayou Texar and Carpenter Creek Watershed Management Plan in Pensacola. Working with hydrologists and ecologists, we are designing landscapes that revive water systems in the same manner of some earlier SCAPE projects (Town Branch Park and Commons in Lexington being a primary example) while also fully embracing southern ecologies. The projects create new public spaces along historic water systems that have been built over, but they also embrace transitional ecotones unique to the Southeast, like hydric hammocks, and celebrate endangered species like the longleaf pine. Ultimately this means a lot of travel and creativity and of course working with local non-profits and others – we aim to piggyback on the work of existing networks where possible.

In Atlanta, Georgia, we are just completing work on a major initiative on the Chattahoochee RiverLands. The working group convened for this project is itself a thing of wonder: municipalities, agencies, private and public groups, nonprofits, and all kinds of regional and local entities coming together around the Chattahoochee River as a central resource. They were the real driving force behind an extensive two-year engagement process resulting in over 75 individual stakeholder and community engagement meetings; we folded these findings into every step of the design process.

At SCAPE we believe there is no single, one-size-fits-all approach to working with communities. You need to respond to local (and historic) conditions and meet people where they are. Sometimes this means realizing that a design firm can't or shouldn't do everything, and that we need to partner with people working locally who better understand the context and how to speak to people effectively. Basic considerations–the timing and location of events, the accessibility of the venue or platform, the availability of translation services, child care, and advance outreach or informational sessions–are all determining factors of an event's success, and who it's successful for. This often means increasing the frequency of meetings to allow more people to attend, but it also means picking and planning the right venue or platform for particular stakeholders, and communicating materials in a way that is accessible to each stakeholder group and translates the plan/projects outcomes relatable to their priorities. We can't assume a single meeting in a given location or one way of presenting a plan or project can effectively engage a diverse or representative demographic. Successful engagement requires multiple means of communication, in multiple formats, and multiple locations.

+ Community is typically a term applied to human social groups that share particular characteristics; however, in your Ecological Citizens exhibition at the 2018 Venice Biennale you extended the definition of community to include nonhuman living entities, such as plant and animal communities. Can you speak to the benefits and challenges of embracing this broader, socio-ecological definition of community in your design practice?

This idea has been a driving force within SCAPE's work for some time: the extension of the word "community" (and "client") to include nonhuman living systems and species. Fostering deeper connections between species–which often means giving them a place to live, treating them as informal "design clients"–is a key mission for the firm. For SCAPE, this has historically happened in watery, porous places: intertidal zones, neglected urban watersheds, etc. For *Ecological Citizens* it was expanded to the regional scale. To design living infrastructure is to invite a whole new palette of underwater places: fin fish, mollusks, crustaceans, and the sediment loads trapped in channelized creeks. If we allow sediment, for instance, to be the primary actor or protagonist in a project, that allows us to rethink overall design priorities, including how we assign value to different aspects of an ecosystem. At the same time, it enlarges our visual vocabulary to include the messy, immersive world of tidal zones and mudflats and all the habitat space therein.

+ Do you think there's a need for landscape architecture curricula to include formal training in community and public engagement? What have you done to address any such shortcomings in your role as director of Columbia University's Urban Design program?

When I took over the reins at Columbia Urban Design I revamped the curriculum in a few key ways. The first was to change the course "Reading New York Urbanism" from a course about technology to a course about the fabric and neighborhoods of New York and for our students to learn what makes a neighborhood, how to interview people, and how to get out and hit the pavement and understand a city through experience and through people, not just as a series of maps or a physical construct. We also redirected the studios to have a research and follow-up context with the Hudson Valley Initiative (to help carry forward and give back to the Hudson Valley Region) and the Center for Resilient Cities and Landscapes (to help follow through on the work of our global studios). We also have amazing faculty who have a lot of experience in community-driven planning processes, and even one faculty member who won an award for inventing social capital credits. So it's an incredible group of teachers and faculty who don't conceive urban design as a sort of master planning endeavor but rather as a process of empowerment, and it is a very special program with graduates who have strong values about the role of cities and landscapes.

+ You're becoming increasingly involved in Green New Deal-related activism – what do you see as landscape architecture's role in relation to community and the aims of the Green New Deal?

I raised a few points in a talk at the University of Pennsylvania titled "Workshopping a Green New Deal" that it's maybe worth reiterating in this context. I agree with Billy Fleming of the McHarg Center and others that it is time to work in a more civic context not just in the context of private practice. I am trying to do this in a number of ways with the McHarg Center, the Landscape Architecture Foundation, and Columbia. Of course, it's helpful for designers to be versed in the broader context of environmental activism and policy – but the primary skill we bring is design thinking. We work with subject matter experts, and the tools we offer–outlining scenarios, tradeoffs, multiple benefits, the lived experience that landscape architects and urban designers have on the built environment–help translate policy into pathways to action. The activist-designer role also straddles all the realities of landscape architecture as a profit-driven business. Often, we are doing our best to incorporate resilient systems even into waterfront development projects in Brooklyn and Queens. It manifests at all scales.

More broadly, the Green New Deal is policy at the federal level – we can't let this go, write this off, or be too cynical (even in light of the coronavirus pandemic) that a federal response is moot. We just cannot accept this. We need a federal response to climate emergency! The Green New Deal forces landscape architects and urban designers to reckon with an entirely different scale, one that has been brought center stage both by the emergent youth climate movement of the past several years and a wealth of dire risk science. We must reckon with climate change at a planetary scale, in terms of gross emissions and irreversibly warming, acidifying oceans – and understand with great urgency that we are operating within a rapidly disappearing carbon budget. Every profession must bring their best to bear. For landscape architects, this is both a design challenge and a communications challenge. We must be vocal, knowledgeable, convincing, and uncompromising.

MARIO MATAMOROS
MISSING COMMON GROUND

Mario Matamoros is an architect and professor at the School of Architecture at Universidad Nacional Autónoma de Honduras where he teaches urban design. A member of the International Working Group of Urban Health at the Interacademy Partnership, his recent research is focused on suburbia, democracy, and urban health.

+ POLITICS, URBAN DESIGN, SOCIAL THEORY

Community, with its Latin root *communis*, refers to the common, the public, shared by all or many. The word embodies a democratic notion where the participation of community members in decisions that affect the community is assumed. But recent decades have witnessed the rendering of facade governments led by the free market and the interests of corporations that, under the flags of progress and (now) sustainability, have orchestrated immense economic deals avoiding critical citizen participation. Political geographer Erik Swyngedouw argues that the *political*–the radical heterogeneity–that constitutes society, has been banned from everyday politics to facilitate the flow of markets and capital.[1] Through neoliberal models of governance-beyond-the-state that internalize private agents in the act of governing and the social manipulation of groups, the Establishment has eradicated the *demos* from the decision-making process, hence reducing the frictions to get "business as usual" done.[2]

While the deregulation process has permitted the privatization of the public, social manipulation applied by the privatized states has served not just to group the factions of dissidence, but also to dangerously radicalize their differences, aggravating discourses of fear and hate toward these groups. One could relate this to the current Honduran political landscape where, in the urge of privatizing the country's services and infrastructure, the government has named opposing factions as the violent enemies of progress and welfare. At least for Hondurans, it seems democracy has unfortunately become more a tool to homogenize and sedate communities than a stage where one can cultivate or recognize difference. For the powers that be, heterogeneity is seen as an antonym to the notion of democracy. If the contemporary condition of politics is that of being subordinated to economic powers and if the city is, as Tom Marble puts it, nothing more than "an archive of successive economies,"[3] then one must wonder what the effects of fake democracy signify in the production of space. In the following, I argue that design is failing to raise social awareness of the spatial impacts of our radicalizing difference, and further, through discussion of local experiences in Honduras, I explore the absence of real democracy in the politics and design of public space.

Simulating Civitas

As fear and crisis dominate the current motives of power, planning, and politics, technocratic governments have, in the absence of democracy, inserted controlling instruments to dissipate unwanted revolts and social awareness. These have facilitated the emergence of managerial models such as the "smart city," a model more concerned with monitoring and controlling public discontent than with creating democratic civic platforms where the negotiations of power can take place. As Mike Crang and Stephen Graham explain, the current tendency to incorporate technology into urban management has saturated our environments with anticipatory technologies.[4] Beyond the incursion of facial recognition devices, surveillance cameras, drones, and heat and noise detectors in urban space, one must visualize other elements the wars on terror and crime have integrated into the cities of the Global South. Cities have been fortified with gated communities, militarily equipped police forces, and barricades to contain potential protests and political uprisings.

The combination of fear and technology in contemporary cities has weakened the notion of community and, as Rem Koolhaas has observed, citizens have been reduced to consumers.[5] The deregulation of politics and the globalization of the economy has decomposed the urban environment in such a way that we only coexist by consuming together in homogenized, sanitized, and controlled places – something Michael Jacobs describes as "apparently happy islands of atmospheric capitalism."[6] Unaware of the implications of economic power in the production of space, urbanists have reduced this concern to a hedonistic approach where planning and design city interventions have facilitated gentrification processes. This has happened at the same pace as diverse communities have been removed from contesting such spaces.

Under such oppressive conditions, urbanism's potentially subversive tools and frameworks have failed to revive communities, and hence the city. Tactical urbanism, for example, has become a trend rather than an efficient instrument to make change possible. One can now relate urban acupuncture with the banal installation of pop-up elements and the painting of insignificant decorations on street surfaces. New hipster-like communities have seen tactical urbanism as an opportunity to conquer deprived neighborhoods with catchy concepts like the "orange economy"[7] or "creative economy" – concepts that sound good but in fact oversimplify the relations and conflicts between economy, politics, and power. In this respect, Reinier De Graaf of OMA believes urbanism is now being produced by consultants other than architects, planners, and landscape architects, arguing that the city is now a domain

of "digital entrepreneurs, asset managers, software vendors, social engineers, real estate moguls, and tech giants."[8] Such a crowded field of innovators has unfortunately withheld the instruments of decision-making from a large group of concerned stakeholders and urban experts. Considering this, one can visualize the contemporary production of civic space as the cold result of big data analyses, its social potential being controlled by technocratic devices hindering civic action, and worse, its design potential ridiculed by mainstream copy-paste interventions which, far from raising or empowering citizens, just mimic cultural liberalization

No One's Square

Although many argue that the Latin-American city was never planned and therefore became a mesh of social problems dominated by inequality, poverty, and vulnerability, Gonzalo Basile maintains that it has indeed been planned, but by the free market.[9] This, among many other implications, has resulted in the configuration and function of civic space being "designed" in accordance with market indicators rather than in reflection of the social needs of people's daily lives. In other words, the city has been planned to fail socially so that it can thrive economically (at least for some).

In his essay "Blood on the Square," architectural historian Steve Basson explains that throughout history, public squares in the hearts of cities have acted as platforms for protest and as places from which to "call for genuine reform."[10] For De Graaf, that city is no more.[11] As Dutch sociologist and criminologist Marc Schuilenberg observes, public space is no longer truly public since it "cannot be defined anymore in terms of socially open-ended space to which no social group can be denied access."[12] Even if we consider that public space was formerly a place where many voices were heard and where great political changes gained momentum, public squares, at least in Honduras, have now been reduced to selfie backdrops. As De Graaf puts it, "public space is experienced as part of a private holiday, it backgrounds a leisure condition, in which the city takes the form of a resort, its history featuring only as a distraction – no longer what anchors us, but what allow us to escape."[13] In other words, the public plaza where locals used to find each other, defy tyranny, and fight for civil rights has been invaded by the things tourists want to see such as al fresco cafés, souvenir stalls, and street artists. One could go so far as to say the square is the new apolitical space of our late-capitalist times. While De Graaf and Schuilenberg seem to argue that our conception of the city and its public space is outdated or romantic, Swyngedouw expresses his faith that this space can be reconfigured politically. He believes that the political occupations of public space that occurred in 2011 in various cities around the globe produced new forms of emancipatory spatialization.[14] Whether or not public space could remain politically relevant to communities and a real *civitas* be achievable in urban spaces designed and run as a financial asset,[15] we must commit to envision a new agora of disagreement and contestation.

In the particular case of Honduras, the marketization of national resources and services has caused a shift in the geographies of power and discontent. The marketization of the city and its agora has relocated political dissent primarily to the internet or, in the worst-case scenario, to violent events occurring in places containing infrastructural elements of logistical importance. In Honduras and many other countries in Latin America, dams, transportation hubs, regional roads, and urban boulevards are increasingly becoming sites of protest and antagonism. This is not because the infrastructures are any more public than city squares (indeed, they are often the result of public–private partnerships and therefore managed by international consortia), but because they are effective in disrupting the city. Outraged communities have understood better than designers and planners that logistics is the new commons.[16] Squares represent no one's interests but those of the tourism industry; they have no political relevance. Infrastructures, on the other hand, epitomize sensible collective interests that result in their politicization, regardless of being public or private domain. They are the new political stages of the community.

This, however, is not what the government and their urban design consultants have in mind when they invite the community to participate in the design process. Since 2014, the Inter-American Development Bank's Emerging and Sustainable Cities Program and the private initiative Vuelve al Centro (Return to the Downtown) have conducted a series of participatory workshops to envision the revitalization of Tegucigalpa's historic downtown through the development of the so-called orange economy. The workshops usually start with the organizers presenting an urban diagnosis exposing the deficiencies and potentials of the city through rough indicators of city performance but lacking statistical evidence of public opinion. At the end of the presentation, they typically

show the best practices to deal with the problems identified in the diagnosis and what things would look like if nothing were to change. After showing a quantitative analysis, the workshop shifts to a qualitative approach as participants are asked to gather in small groups to identify the problems they encounter in the urban realm and to propose respective solutions. The responses are inevitably biased by the previous presentations about problems and solutions and by the fact that the organizers assign one of their own to each group to frame and lead the discussions.

Another fact that aggravates the lack of real dissensus in these workshops is that they are often designed to bring only homogenous interests to the table. While a range of groups (designers, youth, merchants, residents) may be invited to participate, they typically do so in isolated interest-based workshop sessions. By controlling the flow of information and limiting the possible interactions between different interests, participants are neither able to see the whole picture nor have the information needed to meaningfully participate in determining appropriate and inclusive futures for their cities. Participation is in this way used to validate the organizers' predetermined outcomes in what urban theorist Fernando Gaja i Diaz refers to as a protocol of mass therapy.[17]

(Re)designing a Common Ground

We often see how space is conceived and designed with no regard for the social tensions around it, and, paradoxically, how the repression of disagreement as a part of quotidian public life can sometimes lead to more violent events. To activate the commons as a platform of negotiation, we require a design framework that acknowledges the need for antagonism in the public realm. Such a framework would also need to reconsider the dichotomy of public and private, as this separation limits the potential of strategies enabling civic engagement and negotiation in privately owned or managed places. While many design proposals in the urban realm attempt to blur the boundaries between the private and public spheres, I propose that the commons is not about blurring such frontiers but acting consciously upon them. This way, more socially conscious designers could fight against the privatization of the commons, impeding urban design that works to sanitize, control, and dilute civic activism.

Here tactical urbanism has a chance to redeem itself by focusing more on the objects of dissidence–the everyday items

Protest Map of Tegucigalpa
(2009–2019)

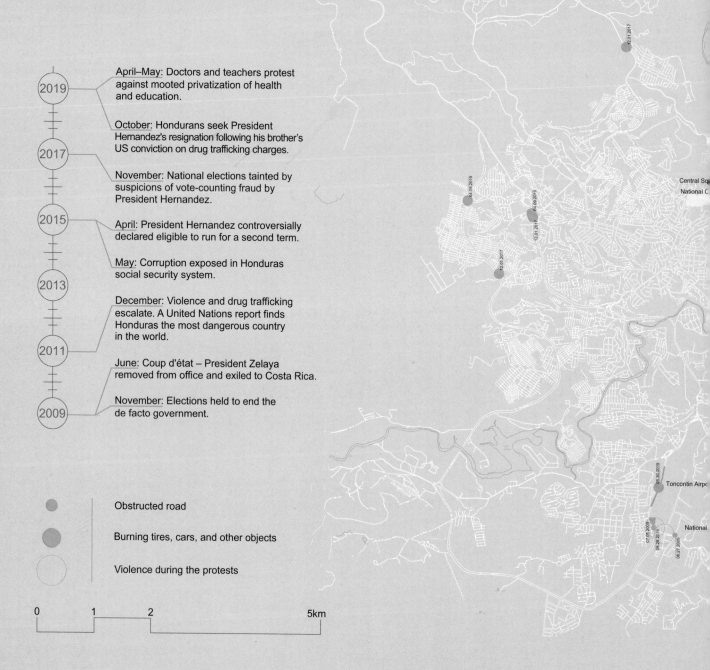

2019

April–May: Doctors and teachers protest against mooted privatization of health and education.

2017

October: Hondurans seek President Hernandez's resignation following his brother's US conviction on drug trafficking charges.

November: National elections tainted by suspicions of vote-counting fraud by President Hernandez.

2015

April: President Hernandez controversially declared eligible to run for a second term.

May: Corruption exposed in Honduras social security system.

2013

December: Violence and drug trafficking escalate. A United Nations report finds Honduras the most dangerous country in the world.

2011

June: Coup d'état – President Zelaya removed from office and exiled to Costa Rica.

2009

November: Elections held to end the de facto government.

Obstructed road

Burning tires, cars, and other objects

Violence during the protests

0   1   2   5km

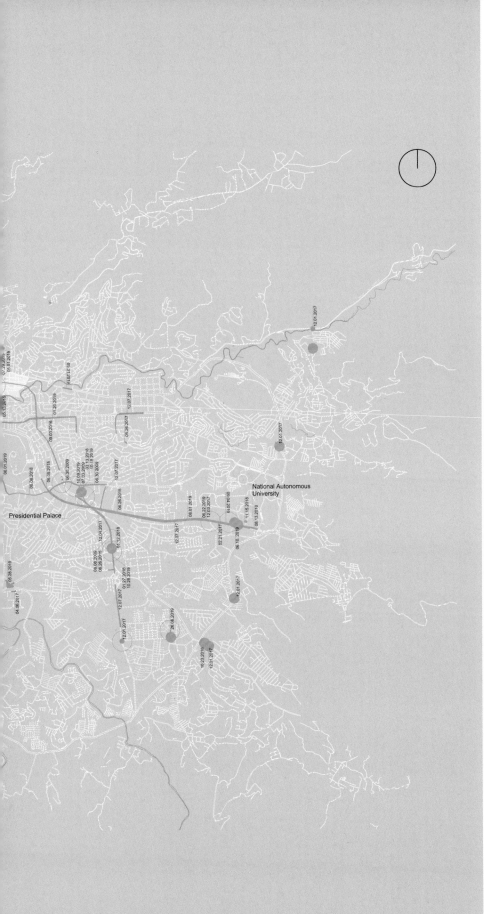

Presidential Palace

National Autonomous University

1 Japhy Wilson & Erik Swyngedouw, *The Post-Political and its Discontents* [Edinburgh University Press, 2014], 4.

2 Mario Matamoros, "The Neoliberal Simplification of Architecture," *Plat Journal* 8 [2019]: 212.

3 Tom Marble, "The Role of Technology in the Evolution of Cities," *MONU* 16 [2012]: 52.

4 Mile Crang & Stephen Graham, "Sentient Cities," *MONU* 16 [2012]: 56–63.

5 Rem Koolhaas, *S, M, L, XL* [The Monacelli Press, 1995], 1260.

6 Michael Jakob, "Landscape Architecture and the 'New Generic,'" [Lecture, Harvard Graduate School of Design, November 16, 2017].

7 The Inter-American Development Bank [IDB] defines orange economy as "the set of activities that in an interlocking way allow for ideas to be transformed into cultural goods and services" with "talent and creativity as leading inputs." See, IDB, "Launching an Orange Future," https://publications.iadb.org/publications/english/document/Launching-an-Orange-Future-Fifteen-Questions-for-Getting-to-Know-the-Creative-Entrepreneurs-of-Latin-America-and-the-Caribbean.pdf.

8 Reinier de Graaf, *Four Walls and a Roof* [Harvard University Press, 2017], 369.

9 Gonzalo Basile, "Urbanismo, Desigualdades y Sistemas de Salud en Latinoamérica y el Caribe; Hacia un Observatorio de la Salud en las Ciudades," [Paper presented at the 1st Latin-American and Caribbean Urban Health Workshop, San Salvador, September 27, 2019].

10 Steve Basson, "Blood on the Square," *LA+ Interdisciplinary Journal of Landscape Architecture* 3 [2016]: 12.

11 De Graaf, *Four Walls and a Roof*, 121.

12 Mark Schuilenberg, "Sweeping Public Space," *Volume* 53 [2018]: 28.

13 De Graaf, *Four Walls and a Roof*, 119.

14 Erik Swyngedouw, "The Velvet Violence of Insurgent Architects," *LA+ Interdisciplinary Journal of Landscape Architecture* 3 [2016]: 30.

15 Ibid., 119.

16 Claire Lyster, "Logistical Hijack," *Volume* 47 [2016]: 47.

17 Fernando Gaja i Diaz, "Urbanismo Concesional: Modernización, Privatización y Cambio de la Hegemonia en la Acción Urbana," *Ciudades* 18, no. 1 [2010]: 109.

18 Ana Medina, "Dissident Micro-Occupations, Architectural Practices, Transforming the Urban Landscape: Istanbul, Hong Kong, Tokyo," *MONU* 17 [2017]: 14.

19 Ibid.

20 Sara Dean, "Protest and Assembly in the Augmented City," https://www.foreground.com.au/politics/protest-and-assembly-in-the-augmented-city/

21 Civil Society Futures, "It's time to Rediscover *Homo Civica*," https://civilsocietyfutures.org/time-rediscover-homo-civica/

22 Ibid.

and infrastructural elements corrupted for the purpose of protest–than on the spaces of dissidence. Occupations like that of Myashita Park in Tokyo (2010) illustrate how small items like plastic boxes, suitcases, bicycle wheels, and traffic cones can be utilized as objects to manifest discontent transforming into speakers, canvases, and rotating banner mechanisms. One could also refer to the pop-up structures that emerged during the 18-day occupation of Istanbul's Gezi Park (2013). During that occupation, protesters used telephone cabins as barricades, a bus as an information center for protestors, and plastic bags were used to make hammocks.[18] Tents were also arranged according to specific group interests and identities enabling informal communal spaces where debate was possible. Finally, the Umbrella Movement in Hong Kong (2014)–an occupation that took over bridges, highways, overpasses, and metro stations–proved how a commonplace object could embody a political message. Umbrellas served both as personal barricades and as a "powerful image of protection and resistance."[19] The impromptu collective use of otherwise unremarkable spatial and ephemeral elements of everyday urban life can, at least for short periods of time, activate new political configurations within a community, bringing to life the heterogeneity of its constituents.

As the city has become increasingly augmented by information and data, our civic actions have too. For example, a group of Detroit activists opposed to "Architectural Imagination"–the 2016 call for the US Pavilion in the Venice Architecture Biennale–created an app, which, through augmented reality, inserted virtual objects such as a graffitied water tower and anti-eviction mural into the pavilion without affecting the physical exhibit. Such an example of digital activism demonstrates how design and virtual augmentation can enable individuals to express and experience a virtual aesthetics of disagreement and negotiation.[20] Another example is *Border Memorial* by artist John Craig Freeman, which, through a digital installation visualizing where migrant workers died while crossing the US-Mexico border, effectively speculates on the potential of design as a way to make visible the forgotten history and spatiality of places charged with political meaning and prone to contestation.

As architect Indy Johar implies in his manifesto *Homo Civica*, a bearable future requires us to rebuild and enlarge the role of the citizen by "embracing the civic agency, capacity, and participation of citizens."[21] To do so, and perhaps recognizing we need a new ground, Johar suggests we need to recreate a liminal space, a platform "beyond the enslavement of our current roles."[22] He describes this as a space of emancipation, a place where we can democratize our capacity to think, discuss, care, and create. Such a conceptualization of democracy being materialized in space necessitates not just communities interested and willing to fulfill such goals, but designers eager to revisit the role of the public and question civic space today. We (designers) must conceptualize new political spaces and objects of disagreement, bridge new forms of negotiation, and create new (and better) narratives of antagonism. For that to be accomplished we must reframe misused methods of planning and design such as tactical urbanism and focus groups, and abandon the empty rhetoric of overoptimistic and oversimplifying plans promoted by governments, investors, and "world-renowned" urban design consultants. Beyond the act of controlling and monitoring, we can improve our use of technologies by facilitating new arenas and aesthetics of contestation. Perhaps we can no longer indulge in the romance of thinking of city squares as public spaces for political emancipation, but we can embrace new sites for contestation. And design can regain relevance in the making of new and better democracies where different communities are empowered and enabled to take back the city.

IMAGE CREDITS